D0549361

Eyewitness
HORSE

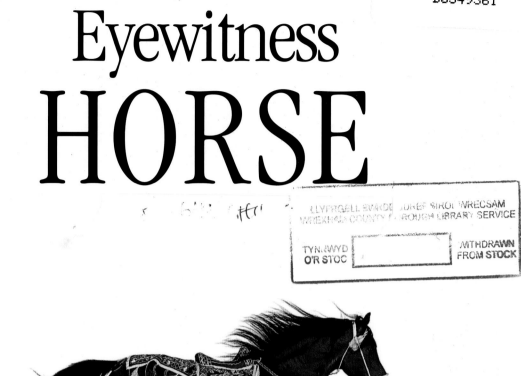

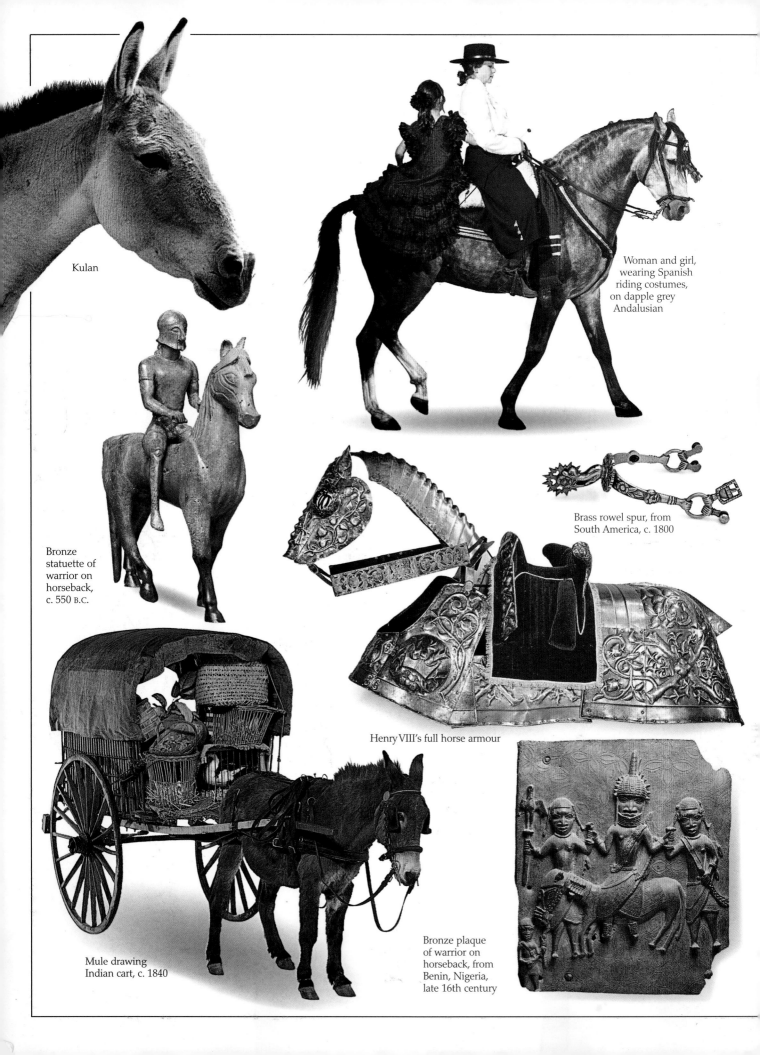

Kulan

Woman and girl,
wearing Spanish
riding costumes,
on dapple grey
Andalusian

Bronze
statuette of
warrior on
horseback,
c. 550 B.C.

Brass rowel spur, from
South America, c. 1800

Henry VIII's full horse armour

Mule drawing
Indian cart, c. 1840

Bronze plaque
of warrior on
horseback, from
Benin, Nigeria,
late 16th century

Eyewitness
HORSE

Foot and two side toes of *Anchitherium* fossil

Old shoe and nails removed from horse's hoof

Written by
JULIET
CLUTTON-BROCK

Mountain zebra

Shoeing a Shire horse

Dapple grey jumping

DK

Drum horse
and rider

LONDON, NEW YORK,
MELBOURNE, MUNICH, and DELHI

Irish donkey
pulling cart, c. 1850

Project editor Marion Dent
Art editor Jutta Kaiser-Atcherley
Senior editor Helen Parker
Senior art editor Julia Harris
Production Louise Barratt
Picture research Diana Morris
Special photography Jerry Young, Karl Shone

THIS EDITION
Editors Susan Malyan, Sue Nicholson,
Victoria Heywood-Dunne, Marianne Petrou
Art editors Rebecca Johns, David Ball
Managing editors Andrew Macintyre, Camilla Hal
Managing art editors Jane Thomas, Martin Wils
Publishing manager Sunita Gahir
Production editors Siu Yin Ho, Andy Hilliard
Production controllers Jenny Jacohy, Pip Tinsl
Picture research Bridget Tily
DK picture library Rose Horridge,
Myriam Megharbi, Emma Shepherd

Two wild Przewalski's horses

Archer on horseback,
c. fifth century BCE.

This Eyewitness ® Guide has been conceived by
Dorling Kindersley Limited and Editions Gallimard

First published in Great Britain in 1992
This revised edition published in 2003, 2008
by Dorling Kindersley Limited,
80 Strand, London WC2R 0RL

2 4 6 8 10 9 7 5 3 1
ED635 – 04/08

Colour reproduction by Colourscan, Singapore
Printed and bound by Leo Paper Products Ltd, China

Discover more at
www.dk.com

French-style barouche, c. 1880

Pair of greys
with English
phaeton, c. 1840

Palomino with
Western-style
bridle and saddle

Contents

Pair of Dutch Gelderlanders
pulling covered waggon

The horse family

HORSES, ASSES, AND ZEBRAS all belong to one family of mammals called the "Equidae". They are called "odd-toed" animals because they only have one hoof on each foot, whereas cows and deer have two hooves and are called "even-toed". The Equidae are classified in the order Perissodactyla with their nearest relatives, the rhinoceroses and tapirs. All members of the horse family (equids) feed by grazing on grasses and shrubs, live in open country, and are fast-running animals that depend on speed to escape from predators. All highly social (pp.12–13), they live in family groups which join together into a herd. They will travel over great distances in search of food or water, or to get away from flies and mosquitoes which plague them in hot weather. Although there is a great variation in size between different breeds of domestic horse (pp.38–41), they all belong to one species – *Equus caballus*. A pony is defined as a horse that has a height of less than 148 cm (14.2 hands/58 in). Various parts of a horse all have different names and are called the "points" of the horse.

"RIDE A COCK-HORSE TO BANBURY CROSS
To see a fine lady upon a white horse …"
Wooden rocking horses with legs on springs, or rockers, have been traditional toys for hundreds of years.

Mane

Withers

Forelock

White blaze

Muzzle

Well-developed neck muscles, used for pulling heavy loads

Ribs

Girth line

Wide rump

Dock

Flank

Thigh

Gaskin

Hock

Point of shoulder

Breast

Elbow

Strong neck

Fetlock

Forearm

A SCOTTISH MINIATURE
The Shetland pony is the smallest of the ancient breeds of pony – this seven-year-old is 81 cm (8 hh/32 in) in height. It is a very hardy animal that requires little food and can carry large loads on bad roads or on the farm (pp.62–63). The original habitat of the Shetland pony was the Shetland Islands, but today the pony can be found in several countries.

Knee

Long, very full tail

Swall hoof

Pastern

Coronet

No forelock

Large ears with dark tips

Heavy head

Short, erect mane

Dark muzzle

Long, erect ears

Typical white muzzle

Pale brown shadow striping between black stripes

Dark muzzle

ASSES AND ZEBRAS
Other than the horse, the other members of the horse family are the Asian wild asses (pp.16–17), the African wild ass (pp.16–17), which is the ancestor of the domestic donkey (pp.24–25), and the zebras (pp.18–19).

Pale underbelly

Kulan – a type of Asian wild ass

Poitou donkey

Common, or plains, zebra mother and foal

Broad back

Very powerful rump

How to measure a horse's height
The height of a horse is measured in "hands". One hand, literally the width of an adult's hand, is equal to 10.16 cm (4 in). If a horse measures 15.2 hh (hands high), then it is 157 cm (62 in) high. This measurement is taken from its feet to the top of its shoulders, which are called the "withers".

Short tail prevents snagging in harness

A GREAT HORSE
The Shire horse was first bred in the English Midlands for work on farms and for pulling great weights (pp.50–53). This breed is distinguished by its huge size and by the long hair, or "feathering", around the feet. The horse shown here, called "King", once held the record for the tallest horse in the world – with a height at the withers of 198 cm (19.2 hh/78 in).

Feathered feet

Huge hoof

A unicorn is a mythical horse that had a long horn growing out of its forehead. In heraldry, this "horse" had a lion's tail, two-toed hooves, and a horn twisted into a spiral.

EUROPEAN TRAVELLERS
Africa has given the world many members of the horse family – from zebras to wild asses. As Europeans explored this vast continent, they brought their domesticated horses with them to use as transport. This elaborate wooden carving of human and animal figures (including horses) was made by Ibo people in Nigeria, West Africa.

How horses evolved

I**T TOOK ABOUT 55 MILLION YEARS** for the present family of horses, asses, and zebras (equids) to evolve from their earliest horse-like ancestor. Originally called *Eohippus*, or "dawn horse" – because it lived during the Eocene period (54 million years ago) – it is now known as *Hyracotherium*. This early horse was not much larger than a hare. It was a "browsing" animal – which fed on leaves and shrubs – and had four hoofed toes on its front feet and three on its hind feet. It lived in the woodlands of Europe, North America, and eastern Asia. Gradually, over millions of years, this small animal evolved into a "grazing" (grass-eating) mammal with three hoofed toes, and later with a single hoof, on all feet. At first, browsing horses, like *Mesohippus* and then *Parahippus*, had low-crowned teeth (pp.10–11), but during the later Miocene period (20 million years ago) grasslands began to replace the woodlands in North America. In adapting to this new environment, ancestral horses evolved longer limbs that enabled them to range over a wide area in search of pasture and to escape from predators. At the same time, their teeth became high-crowned in order to adapt to their diet of tough grasses. The first grazing horse was *Merychippus*, but eventually it was replaced by *Pliohippus*, the first one-toed horse. This gave rise to *Equus* during the Pleistocene (about two million years ago).

Side toe

Hoof of side toe

Main hoof-core

Side view of left hind foot of *Hipparion*

Left side toe

Right side hoof

Hoof of small side toe

Main hoof-core

Front view of hind foot of *Hipparion*

Nasal bone

Incisor tooth

Ear bone

SOUTH AMERICAN HORSE

This is the skeleton of *Hippidion*, an extinct one-toed equid that evolved in Central America and then spread into South America. Its descendant, *Onoluppidium*, survived in South America until at least 12,000 years ago, when their extinction may have been hastened by the first human hunters moving through the continent at the end of the Ice Age.

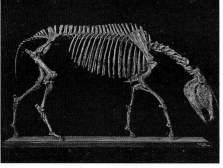

LAST OF THE THREE-TOED HORSES

Hipparion (side view of skull, above) was the last of the three-toed equids. It was a very successful grazer with high-crowned teeth and its fossil remains have been found in many parts of Europe, Asia, and Africa. *Hipparion* did not finally become extinct in Africa until about 125,000 years ago.

Incisor for cutting food

Lost incisor

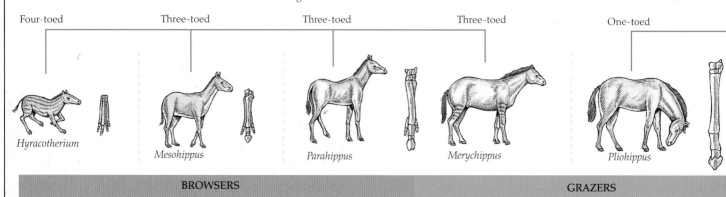

Four-toed	Three-toed	Three-toed	Three-toed	One-toed
Hyracotherium	*Mesohippus*	*Parahippus*	*Merychippus*	*Pliohippus*

BROWSERS

GRAZERS

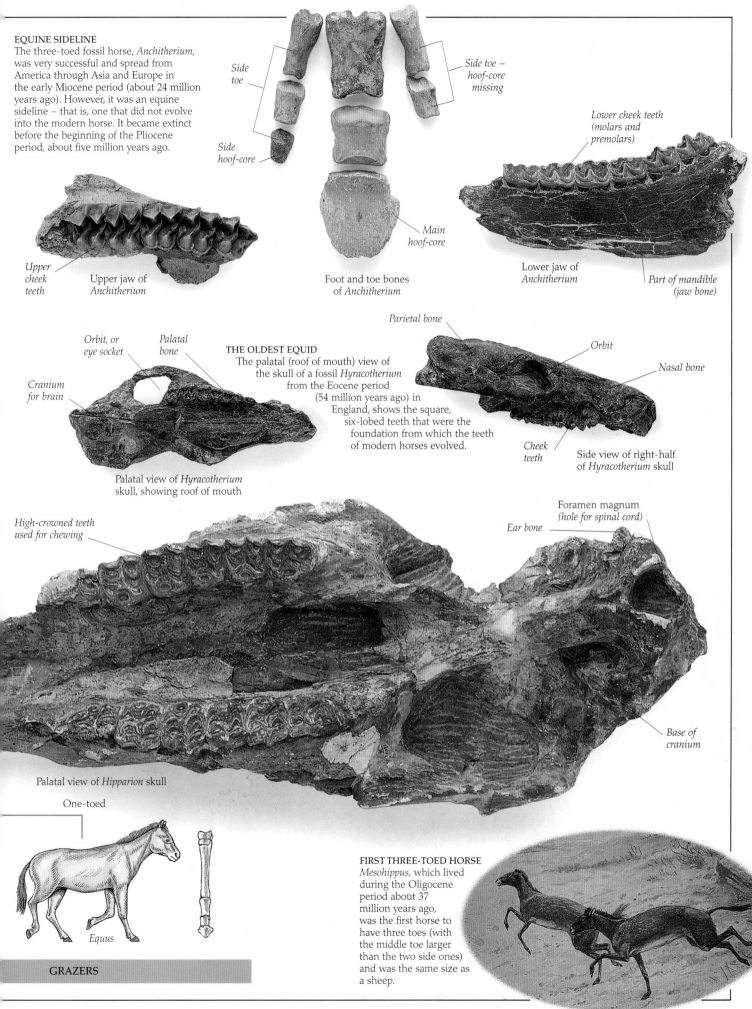

EQUINE SIDELINE
The three-toed fossil horse, *Anchitherium*, was very successful and spread from America through Asia and Europe in the early Miocene period (about 24 million years ago). However, it was an equine sideline – that is, one that did not evolve into the modern horse. It became extinct before the beginning of the Pliocene period, about five million years ago.

Side toe

Side toe – hoof-core missing

Side hoof-core

Main hoof-core

Foot and toe bones of *Anchitherium*

Lower cheek teeth (molars and premolars)

Lower jaw of *Anchitherium*

Part of mandible (jaw bone)

Upper cheek teeth

Upper jaw of *Anchitherium*

Orbit, or eye socket

Palatal bone

Cranium for brain

THE OLDEST EQUID
The palatal (roof of mouth) view of the skull of a fossil *Hyracotherium* from the Eocene period (54 million years ago) in England, shows the square, six-lobed teeth that were the foundation from which the teeth of modern horses evolved.

Parietal bone

Orbit

Nasal bone

Cheek teeth

Side view of right-half of *Hyracotherium* skull

Palatal view of *Hyracotherium* skull, showing roof of mouth

High-crowned teeth used for chewing

Foramen magnum (hole for spinal cord)

Ear bone

Base of cranium

Palatal view of *Hipparion* skull

One-toed

Equus

GRAZERS

FIRST THREE-TOED HORSE
Mesohippus, which lived during the Oligocene period about 37 million years ago, was the first horse to have three toes (with the middle toe larger than the two side ones) and was the same size as a sheep.

Cranium (of skull)

Eye socket

Upper molar

Nasal bone

Upper premolar

Incisor, used for cutting food

Lower premolar

Lower jaw, or mandible

Atlas

Axis

Lower molar

Neck vertebra

Incisor teeth of this 20-yr-old horse angled forwards, showing old age

Scapula, or shoulder blade

Humerus

LONG IN THE TOOTH
As a horse grows older, the shape of its incisors changes from oval to round to triangular and then a flattened four-sided shape. Also with age, a horse's gums recede (so that it becomes "long in the tooth") and its teeth wear down. With all these indicators, experts can estimate how old a horse is.

Bones and teeth

THE SKELETON OF ALL MEMBERS of the horse family is built for speed and stamina. All wild equids range over huge areas of open grassland and, to escape from predators, they gallop fast and have extraordinarily sharp eyesight. The skull of the horse has to be very long to contain the great battery of grinding teeth that are needed for chewing grass. The vertebral column keeps the back rigid, the rib cage protects the heart and lungs, and the limb bones are greatly extended. A distinguishing feature of the equids is that they run on only a single toe. This is equivalent to the third finger, or toe, of a human, while toes two and four are reduced to thin splint bones, and toes one and five are lost altogether. When a foal is born, it may be toothless, but the milk, or baby, teeth erupt through the soft jaw bones. Milk teeth are temporary and, in time, are replaced by adult, or permanent, teeth. An adult equid normally has 40 teeth – 12 incisors, 4 canines, 12 premolars, and 12 molars – but in the female the canines are very small. As horses age, their teeth gradually wear down, change shape, and become very discoloured.

CLASSIC SKELETON
In 1766, the English artist George Stubbs (1724–1806) published a book entitled *The Anatomy of the Horse*, which is still used as a classic work of reference more than 200 years later. In order to show the horse's bone construction accurately, he had to dissect a great number of horses.

Radius

Knee

Metacarpal, or front cannon, bone

First phalanx, or long pastern bone

Second phalanx, or short pastern bone

Hoof

Skeleton of a racehorse

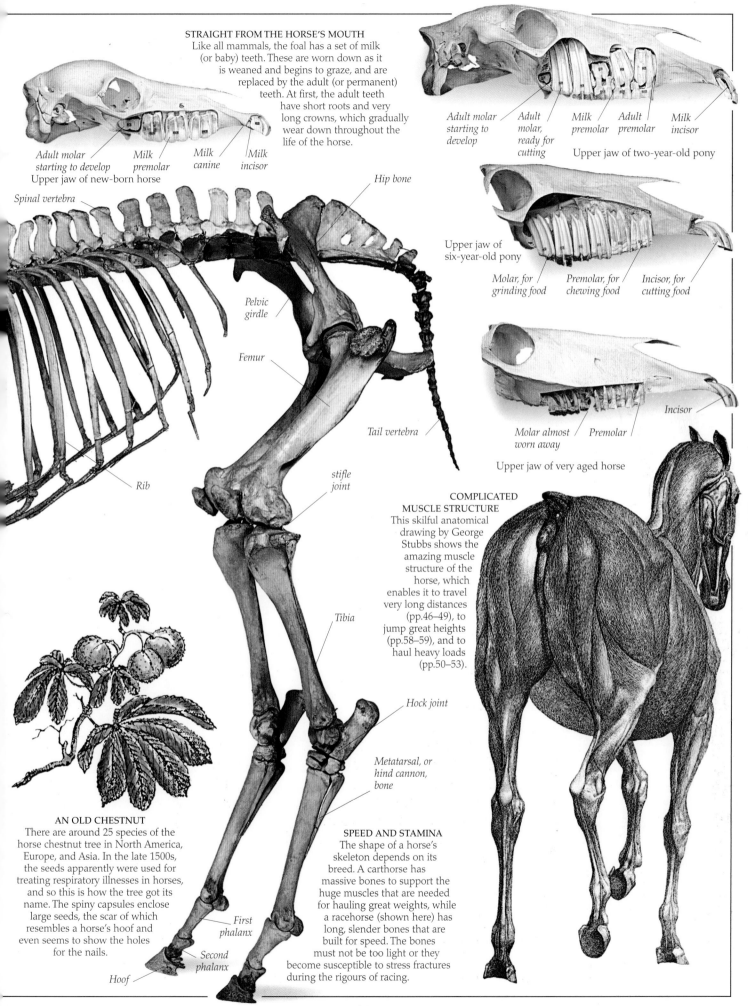

STRAIGHT FROM THE HORSE'S MOUTH
Like all mammals, the foal has a set of milk (or baby) teeth. These are worn down as it is weaned and begins to graze, and are replaced by the adult (or permanent) teeth. At first, the adult teeth have short roots and very long crowns, which gradually wear down throughout the life of the horse.

Adult molar starting to develop
Milk premolar
Milk canine
Milk incisor

Upper jaw of new-born horse

Adult molar starting to develop
Adult molar, ready for cutting
Milk premolar
Adult premolar
Milk incisor

Upper jaw of two-year-old pony

Upper jaw of six-year-old pony

Molar, for grinding food
Premolar, for chewing food
Incisor, for cutting food

Molar almost worn away
Premolar
Incisor

Upper jaw of very aged horse

Hip bone

Spinal vertebra

Pelvic girdle

Femur

Tail vertebra

stifle joint

Rib

Tibia

Hock joint

Metatarsal, or hind cannon, bone

COMPLICATED MUSCLE STRUCTURE
This skilful anatomical drawing by George Stubbs shows the amazing muscle structure of the horse, which enables it to travel very long distances (pp.46–49), to jump great heights (pp.58–59), and to haul heavy loads (pp.50–53).

AN OLD CHESTNUT
There are around 25 species of the horse chestnut tree in North America, Europe, and Asia. In the late 1500s, the seeds apparently were used for treating respiratory illnesses in horses, and so this is how the tree got its name. The spiny capsules enclose large seeds, the scar of which resembles a horse's hoof and even seems to show the holes for the nails.

First phalanx

Second phalanx

Hoof

SPEED AND STAMINA
The shape of a horse's skeleton depends on its breed. A carthorse has massive bones to support the huge muscles that are needed for hauling great weights, while a racehorse (shown here) has long, slender bones that are built for speed. The bones must not be too light or they become susceptible to stress fractures during the rigours of racing.

Senses and behaviour

ROLLING OVER
This pony is having a good roll, which is an important part of grooming. It relaxes the muscles and helps to remove loose hair, dirt, and parasites.

HORSES, ASSES, AND ZEBRAS all have more highly developed senses of sight, hearing, and scent than humans. The characteristic long face of the horse is necessary not only for the large teeth but because it contains the sensitive organs of smell. The eyes are set far up in the skull and are positioned on the sides of the head, so the horse has good all-round vision, even when it is grazing. The ears are large, and in the asses very long, so that they can be moved around and pointed towards the slightest sound. By nature the horse is a herd animal showing great affection towards other members of its group, and this loyalty is easily transferred to its human owner. Once this bond is developed, the horse will try very hard to follow commands, however harsh. As a result, horses have been cruelly used but also deeply loved, possibly more than any other animal in human history. Despite their close association with humans, the domestic horse and donkey still retain the instincts and natural behavioural patterns of their wild ancestors. They will defend their territory and suckle their foals in just the same way as will the wild horse and the wild ass, and they will always need companionship.

Ears pointing back show submission or fear

Ears pointing forwards show interest in surroundings

One ear forward, one ear back shows uncertainty

TWO-WAY STRETCH
An equid's ears have a dual role – to pick up sounds and to transmit visual signals. If a mule (shown here) puts its ears back, it is frightened or angry. If forwards, then it will be interested in what is happening around it, such as the clatter of a food bucket. One ear forward and one back means it is not sure what will happen next.

Laid-back ears showing anger

Kick threat

KULAN'S KICK THREAT
The laid-back ears and threatening kicks show that these kulans, or onagers (pp.16–17), are not getting along too well.

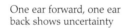

Zebra calling, responding to the threat from another male

PROTECTING TERRITORY AND FAMILY
Fighting by rearing and stabbing with their front hooves is natural to all equids. However, they may prefer to settle their differences by threats with their ears, tails, and feet, and by using other body language. Stallions will fight over territory or to protect their mares, as shown by these Icelandic ponies.

Cartoon shows lead horse ignoring his driver's commands and taking the liberty of stopping for a drink

FLEHMEN REACTION
By pulling back his lips and drawing air in over his vomero-nasal, or Jacobson's, organ after smelling a mare's urine, this stallion is testing whether she is ready to be mated – that is, whether she is on heat ("in oestrus"). This is called the flehmen reaction.

Bite given to unfamiliar horse

A BITE THREAT
These Przewalski's horses (pp.20–21), from two different herds, are trying to show who is the more important, or "dominant", with one horse showing a bite threat to the other. The attacking horse's neck is thrust forward and it is trying to bite its opponent.

THE BEST OF FRIENDS
Two horses will often stand close together, head to tail, nuzzling each other's manes and backs, thus establishing their relationship. The frequency of these grooming and cleaning sessions varies from season to season, but they usually last around three minutes.

Ears laid back showing shock of bite attack

Mares and foals

A MARE, OR MOTHER HORSE, ASS, OR ZEBRA, usually gives birth to one very well-developed foal, after a carrying-time ("gestation period") of about 11 months or a little longer. The mares mate with a stallion within a few days of giving birth, so all the foals are born in spring when there is plenty of grass. The gestation period is long because the mother must produce a healthy foal (or very rarely twins) that is strong enough to keep up with the moving herd as soon as it is born. This is necessary because asses, zebras, and horses are all grazers that live on open grasslands where food can be scarce, and young animals could be an easy target for large predators, such as lions in Africa. The foal is on its feet an hour after birth and, although the mare will continue to suckle her foal for up to a year, it will begin to graze after a few weeks. Between the ages of one and four years, a female foal is called a "filly" and a male foal a "colt". In the wild, fillies and colts will leave their mothers' herds and form new groups of their own when they mature.

A PREGNANT PALOMINO
This Palomino (pp.38–39) shows from her large belly that she will soon give birth. Pony and feral (pp.36–37) mares tend to give birth quickly, but highly bred horses usually need to be keenly watched in case something goes wrong.

A NEW-BORN FOAL
This mare is resting for a few minutes after giving birth to her foal, which still has part of the birth, or amniotic, sac over its back. Soon the foal will kick free from its mother, breaking off the umbilical cord that has provided nourishment up to now in the uterus (womb).

LICKING INTO SHAPE
The mare has got to her feet and removes the birth sac by licking the foal all over. This also helps strengthen the foal's circulation and breathing.

Foal's erect ears showing alertness

MOTHER AND FOAL
It will take almost three years for the young foal of this common zebra (pp.18–19) to become as large as its mother. The family bonds of zebras are very strong and all the adults combine to protect their foals from danger.

Mother nudging foal away from danger

Six-year-old common zebra mother and three-month-old foal

THE FIRST DRINK
As soon as it can stand, the foal will search for the mother's teats between her hind legs and will begin to suck. The first milk is called the "colostrum" and it helps the foal build up life-long immunity to disease.

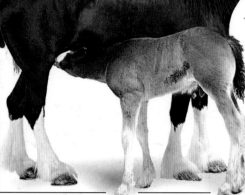

STANDING ON ITS OWN FOUR FEET
While the mother looks around for danger, the foal takes its first faltering steps.

WATCH OUT!
Although this Shire mare (pp.50–53) is descended from horses that have been domesticated for thousands of years (pp.22–23), she still has the instincts of her wild ancestors and will be constantly on guard against possible danger to her foal.

Alert ears listening out for danger

KEEPING UP
A foal is on its feet within an hour of birth and it must try to keep up with its mother – particularly in the wild.

Height at withers 180 cm (17.3hh/71 in)

Mother's muzzle protecting foal

Height at withers 117 cm (11.2 hh/ 46 in)

Ten-year-old Shire mother and her five-week-old foal

... AND SO TO BED
Like all babies, a foal needs a great deal of rest, but it can get to its feet very quickly in case of danger.

Wild asses

THERE ARE THREE SPECIES of wild ass and they are no more closely related to each other than the horse is to the zebra. They can interbreed, but their off-spring will be infertile (pp.18–19). The three species are the true wild ass of Africa (*Equus africanus*), which until recently ranged over the Sahara desert in North Africa, and the two species of Asian wild asses – the onager (*Equus hemionus*) from the Middle East and northwest India, and the kiang (*Equus kiang*) from the Tibetan plateau, north of the Himalayas. Of these three species, it is the African wild ass that is the ancestor of the domestic donkey (pp.24–25). All wild asses look very similar, with quite a heavy head, long ears, a short mane, no forelock, slender legs, and a wispy tail. The African wild ass is greyish in colour, with a white belly and a dark stripe along its back, and it often has horizontal stripes around its legs and a black stripe over its shoulders. The Asian wild asses are redder in colour, but they never have leg or shoulder stripes, although they do have a dark line along their backs. All wild asses are adapted for life in the arid, stony environment of the semi-deserts and mountain plateaus of Africa and Asia, where they graze on thornbushes and dry grass. Today, all wild asses are in danger of extinction from loss of their habitat and over-hunting by humans.

FIRST CATCH YOUR ONAGER
The above scenes of catching wild onagers alive, c. 645 BCE, are from the stone friezes that adorned the palace of Nineveh in Assyria. These Syrian onagers (now extinct) were perhaps being caught for cross-breeding (pp.26–27) with domestic donkeys or horses.

Long, wispy tail

PRESERVATION
Until recently, there were several races of African wild asses. The Somali wild ass (*Equus africanus somaliensis*), the only African ass still to survive in the wild, has stripes round its legs usually, but not on its shoulders. These asses have been taken to a wildlife reserve in Israel to try to save the species, whose home is in Ethiopia and Somalia.

Slender, pale-coloured leg

NOW EXTINCT
The Nubian wild ass (*Equus africanus africanus*) is now extinct. It differed from the Somali ass in having a very short, dark stripe across its shoulders, but no horizontal stripes on its legs.

INDIAN ONAGERS

The Indian onager, or khur (*Equus hemionus khur*), inhabits the hot, dry Thar Desert of northwest India. Like all equids, khurs live in social groups with an old female as the leader of the herd. Except in early summer, during mating time, the adult males live in separate herds from the females.

Large ears with dark tips

No forelock

Heavy head

Short, erect, mid-brown mane

Dark stripe along back

Dark muzzle

PERSIAN ASS

The ghor-khar, or Persian onager (*Equus hemionus onager*), used to live in huge herds that migrated across the deserts in Iran, but today only a very few animals survive in the wild. The onager can gallop at a speed of 48 kph (30 mph) for a long time and can jump over rocks nearly 2 m (7 ft) high.

THE KULAN

These onagers belong to a subspecies, or race, called the kulan (*Equus hemionus kulan*). In the wild, they live in small numbers in the deserts of Turkmenistan, that is east of the Caspian Sea. Kulans are 112–122 cm (11–12 hh/44–48 in) in height. In winter they grow a very thick, yellowish-brown coat which protects them from the icy winds blowing from the mountains. None of the onagers, or the kiang, has ever been domesticated, although it is probable that in the ancient civilizations of the Near East, onagers were crossed with donkeys and horses to produce strong hybrids (pp. 26–27).

Pale, almost white underbelly

NEARLY EXTINCT

The kiang (*Equus kiang*), or Tibetan wild ass, is the largest of all the asses – with a height of over 142 cm (14 hh/56 in). Kiangs are sacred to the Tibetans, but they have been nearly exterminated by hunting and habitat loss.

Queen Puabi's rein ring, made of gold and silver and topped with an onager – part of a chariot harness in the royal tombs at Ur in ancient Mesopotamia, c. 2500 BCE.

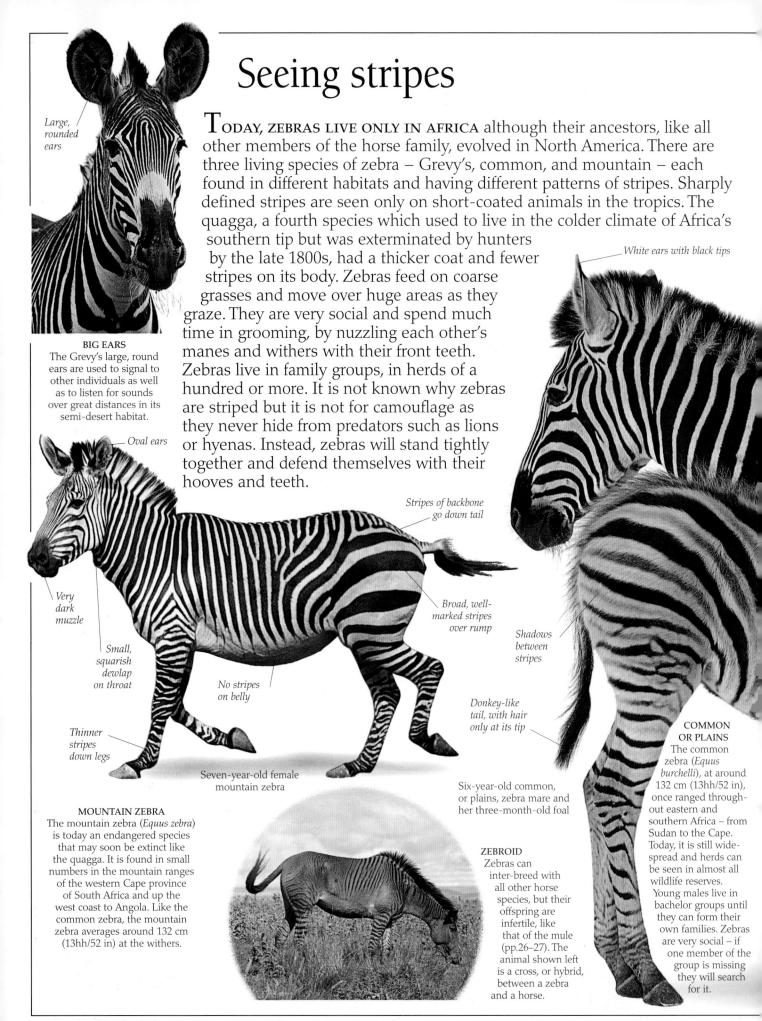

Seeing stripes

TODAY, ZEBRAS LIVE ONLY IN AFRICA although their ancestors, like all other members of the horse family, evolved in North America. There are three living species of zebra – Grevy's, common, and mountain – each found in different habitats and having different patterns of stripes. Sharply defined stripes are seen only on short-coated animals in the tropics. The quagga, a fourth species which used to live in the colder climate of Africa's southern tip but was exterminated by hunters by the late 1800s, had a thicker coat and fewer stripes on its body. Zebras feed on coarse grasses and move over huge areas as they graze. They are very social and spend much time in grooming, by nuzzling each other's manes and withers with their front teeth. Zebras live in family groups, in herds of a hundred or more. It is not known why zebras are striped but it is not for camouflage as they never hide from predators such as lions or hyenas. Instead, zebras will stand tightly together and defend themselves with their hooves and teeth.

Large, rounded ears

BIG EARS
The Grevy's large, round ears are used to signal to other individuals as well as to listen for sounds over great distances in its semi-desert habitat.

Oval ears

Very dark muzzle

Small, squarish dewlap on throat

Thinner stripes down legs

Stripes of backbone go down tail

Broad, well-marked stripes over rump

No stripes on belly

Seven-year-old female mountain zebra

MOUNTAIN ZEBRA
The mountain zebra (*Equus zebra*) is today an endangered species that may soon be extinct like the quagga. It is found in small numbers in the mountain ranges of the western Cape province of South Africa and up the west coast to Angola. Like the common zebra, the mountain zebra averages around 132 cm (13hh/52 in) at the withers.

White ears with black tips

Shadows between stripes

Donkey-like tail, with hair only at its tip

Six-year-old common, or plains, zebra mare and her three-month-old foal

ZEBROID
Zebras can inter-breed with all other horse species, but their offspring are infertile, like that of the mule (pp.26–27). The animal shown left is a cross, or hybrid, between a zebra and a horse.

COMMON OR PLAINS
The common zebra (*Equus burchelli*), at around 132 cm (13hh/52 in), once ranged through-out eastern and southern Africa – from Sudan to the Cape. Today, it is still wide-spread and herds can be seen in almost all wildlife reserves. Young males live in bachelor groups until they can form their own families. Zebras are very social – if one member of the group is missing they will search for it.

Dorsal, or back stripe, is broad and black

Very narrow stripes on face

GREVY'S ZEBRA

Grevy's zebra (*Equus grevyi*) is the most northern of the species and lives in small numbers in the semi-desert areas of Kenya, Ethiopia, and Somalia. It is the largest of the zebras, with an average height of 142–152 cm (14–15 hh/56–60 in). It is not closely related to the other zebras and is considered to be a relic of more primitive members of the horse family.

Rounded ears

No forelock on head

V-shaped, brown patch on nose

Very tall, erect mane

White on either side of black dorsal stripe

Narrow, closely spaced black stripes on a white background, especially over the withers

White underbelly

Two female Grevy's zebras, aged three to four years

Broad hooves

Stripes go down legs, ending in black coronet, next to hoof

Pale brown shadow striping between black stripes

Black dorsal stripe becomes thinner down the tail, with stripes on either side

Stripes bend round becoming horizontal over haunches

White inside of leg with no stripes

THE QUAGGA

Early explorers in southern Africa found herds of more than 100 quaggas (*Equus quagga*) on their yearly migrations to different grazing ground. Gradually they were reduced in numbers by indiscriminate hunting; the last wild quaggas were shot in 1861. Efforts are now being made to recreate the quagga by selectively breeding plains zebras.

ZEDONK

Another type of cross-breeding – between a zebra and a donkey – can result in pale brown-coloured animals with very fine stripes, such as these zedonks from Zimbabwe in central-southern Africa. Many zoos around the world carry out successful cross-breeding programmes.

Ancient ancestors

Fossil evidence tells us that at the end of the last Ice Age 10,000 years ago (pp.8–9), there must have been millions of horses living wild all over Europe, as well as in northern and Central Asia. These animals belonged to one species, called *Equus ferus*, that roamed in herds over the grasslands and probably migrated for hundreds of miles each year. As the climate changed, the grasslands were replaced by forests, and the horses dwindled in numbers from loss of their habitat and from extensive hunting by humans. By 4,000 years ago there were very few wild horses left in Europe, although two subspecies of wild horse – in Russia, the tarpan (*Equus ferus ferus*), and in Mongolia, Przewalski's horse (*Equus ferus przewalskii*) – survived until comparatively recently. Around 6,000 years ago, the first wild horses were being tamed and domesticated in Asia and eastern Europe and they soon spread westwards (pp.22–23). All the domestic horses in the world today are descended from these domesticated ancestors and they are classified in one species, called *Equus caballus*.

EXTINCT WILD HORSE
Many 18th-century travellers to the Russian steppes described herds of small wild horses, some of which were probably feral (pp.36–37). The last tarpans died out in the early 1800s. In Poland today, ponies very like the tarpan have been recreated by breeding from primitive breeds, such as the Konik.

Height range at withers of 132–142 cm (13–14 hh/ 52–56 in)

Short mane

Short forelock

AN ANCIENT ENGLISH PONY
The Exmoor pony is an ancient breed that closely resembles the extinct tarpan, or wild pony of eastern Europe. The ponies live in feral herds on Exmoor in southwest England.

Light-coloured, mealy muzzle, typical of wild horse

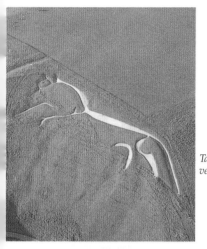

SACRED WHITE HORSE
White horses were sacred animals to the Celts who lived in western Europe around 500 BCE. Around that time, this impression of a horse was scraped out from the white chalk hills at Uffington in Oxfordshire, southern England.

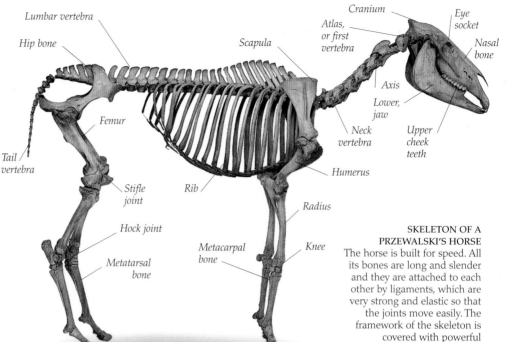

Lumbar vertebra

Hip bone

Scapula

Cranium

Atlas, or first vertebra

Eye socket

Nasal bone

Axis

Lower, jaw

Femur

Neck vertebra

Upper cheek teeth

Tail vertebra

Stifle joint

Rib

Humerus

Hock joint

Radius

Metatarsal bone

Metacarpal bone

Knee

SKELETON OF A PRZEWALSKI'S HORSE
The horse is built for speed. All its bones are long and slender and they are attached to each other by ligaments, which are very strong and elastic so that the joints move easily. The framework of the skeleton is covered with powerful muscles and very little fat.

PRZEWALSKI'S HORSES
Wild horses were found living on the steppes of Mongolia by Russian travellers in the 1880s. A few were brought to Europe, where they bred well in zoos, and were later taken to America. Przewalski's horses have been extinct in the wild since the 1960s, but now they are being reintroduced to Mongolia from herds bred in captivity.

Long, shaggy tail

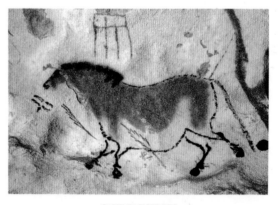

CAVE PAINTINGS
This wild horse (*Equus ferus*) was painted on a wall in the famous caves at Lascaux in France by hunting people towards the end of the last Ice Age, about 14,000 years ago.

WILD AFRICAN ASS
The African wild ass (*Equus africanus*) is the ancestor of all domestic donkeys (pp. 24–25). It is still found in very small numbers in the eastern Sahara but it is in danger of extinction.

Group of Przewalski's horses

Horses in history

THE EARLIEST RELIABLE EVIDENCE for the domestication of the horse comes from the Ukraine, where people lived by herding horses and cattle on the grass steppes 6,000 years ago. At the same time, the African wild ass (pp.16–17) was being domesticated in ancient Egypt and Arabia. At first horses and asses were not usually ridden, but were harnessed in a pair to a cart, or chariot. Soon chariots became the status symbols of kings, who rode in them to battle, in royal parades, and for hunting. By the time of Homer, the Greek poet in eighth century BCE, the riding of horses and donkeys had become a common means of travel (pp.46–49), but chariots were still used for warfare (pp.42–45). In the classical period of civilization, the ancient Greeks and Romans built special arenas and tracks for chariot races, which provided high drama for the crowds who watched these sporting events, involving riders, drivers, and horses (pp.59–61).

THE END OF THE DAY
This horse's head from the Parthenon marbles (fifth century BCE) in Athens, Greece, is one of the greatest sculptures of all time. Legend has it that a team of horses would pull the Sun's chariot to the sea each day to create the sunset. The exhaustion of this extreme effort shows on the horse's face.

ROYAL STANDARD
This very early representation of donkeys harnessed to a four-wheeled cart is on the mosaic decoration of a box – the Standard of Ur – from the royal tombs of Ur in ancient Mesopotamia (c. 2500 BCE).

FLYING THROUGH THE AIR
Pegasus was a mythical horse with wings who, according to the ancient Greeks, had sprung from the blood of Medusa when Perseus, a son of Zeus, cut off her head. The horse flew up to join the gods, but was caught by Athena, the goddess of wisdom, and tamed with a golden bridle. This exquisite engraving of Pegasus is on a bronze cista, or toilet-box, made by the Etruscans, c. 300 BCE.

READY FOR WAR
This terracotta model from Cyprus probably represents an Assyrian warrior, seventh century BCE. The man carries a shield and is ready for battle. His horse has a breastplate and a war-like headdress.

HALF MAN, HALF HORSE
The myth of the centaurs – half men and half horses – may have arisen when people in ancient Greece saw the horsemen of Thessaly. Because they were unfamiliar with men on horseback, they believed they were seeing a new form of being. Shown here is a scene from the epic battles between the wild and lawless centaurs and the Lapiths of northern Greece which appears in the sculptures in the Parthenon, fifth century BCE.

THE FOUR HORSES OF VENICE

Thought to be the work of fourth-century BCE Greek sculptor, Lysippus, these magnificent bronze horses were taken from Constantinople (now Istanbul) in 1204 CE to the San Marco Basilica in Venice. Prior to this they had been in Rome. In 1797, Napoleon took the sculptures to Paris and in 1815 the horses were returned to Venice.

BRAND MARK

Brands on horses (pp.40–41) have been used as proof of ownership for more than 2,000 years. The hunting scene (above) is from a mosaic pavement (c. late fifth or sixth century BCE) discovered at Carthage (a city founded by the Phoenicians near modern-day Tunis). This mosaic from North Africa shows a favourite pastime of wealthy landowners – hunting.

SURPRISE!

During the Trojan War, c. 1184 BCE, the Greeks invaded the city of Troy by hiding soldiers in a huge, wooden horse they had built. The Trojans, believing the Greeks had abandoned the horse, wheeled it into the city. Then the Greeks leapt out and opened the city gates to let in the conquering army.

A BIT OF A TANG

The people of China have always had a great respect for their horses. During the Tang Dynasty (618–907 CE), many earthenware models of horses were produced that are of great artistic value today. The cobalt-blue glaze was very rare and expensive to produce at that time, because cobalt was imported only in very small quantities. This figure would have been moulded in several parts and then joined together as a whole.

Donkey work

THE DOMESTICATED ASS, OR DONKEY (*Equus asinus*), is descended from the African wild ass (*Equus africanus*, pp.16–17), which lives in the hot, dry deserts of the Sahara and Arabia. Because of this harsh environment, the donkey has developed great strength, stamina, and endurance to carry heavy loads over long distances on little food and water. In the wild, donkey foals have to develop quickly so that they can keep up with the herd, as it travels great distances in search of edible bushes and grass. Female donkeys, or jennies, carry their foals for 12 months before they are born – a gestation period of two months more than the female horse (pp.14–15). In the desert and on stony ground the donkey's small neat hooves are kept evenly worn down, but they will grow and must be filed if the animal is kept on soft grass. Like all members of the horse family, the donkey is a social animal and needs to live with other animals if it is to thrive.

JESUS ON A DONKEY
When Jesus was born the donkey was the usual means of transport in Jerusalem, which is why the baby Jesus is always portrayed with his mother on a donkey, being led by Joseph. The "cross" on a donkey's back – a dark stripe along the backbone and a horizontal band across the shoulders – combined with the fact that Jesus rode a donkey on the first Palm Sunday, made people believe that these hairs had healing powers.

ANDALUSIAN GOATHERD
In Andalusia in southwestern Spain, donkeys are still used for herding and farm work. This family is travelling by donkey to take their goats to new pastures.

GREEK HARVEST
In Greece, until recently, it was a common sight to see donkeys threshing grain. By walking round and round in a circle, the donkeys' hooves separate the seeds from the husks.

WATER, WATER
Water is the most precious of all resources in desert countries and it often has to be fetched from far away. This North African woman from Tunisia is carrying her baby and leading her donkey, loaded with water jars.

Rein

Breeching straps (that go around animal's haunches)

Wooden shaft

Footstand for stepping up into cart

Mid-19th-century English donkey cart

Long ears help keep donkey cool

Lighter baby or juvenile coat on back

Darker adult coat, like his father's, now visible at first moulting

Typical white muzzle

POITOU DONKEYS
In the Poitou region of France and in Spain, for hundreds of years there has been a tradition of breeding very large donkeys which are used for mating with female horses, to produce giant mules (pp.26–27) for farm work, in the same way as cart horses were used in more northern countries. Poitou donkeys stand about 142 cm (14 hh/56 in) at the shoulder, or withers, making them the world's largest donkeys. They also have very long, dark, shaggy coats.

White underbelly

Long, slender legs

A family group: five-year-old father, nine-year-old mother, and eleven-month-old son

This poor old donkey has had a hard working life and now deserves a peaceful retirement

AFRICAN DONKEYS
These donkeys are drinking from a waterhole in Kenya where they are living semi-wild on a ranch. They must fend for themselves and learn to keep away from leopards, hyenas, and other predators, just as other wild animals have to do.

Terret

Rein ring

Bridle

Decorated brow band

Blinker

Nose band

Bit

Collar

Trace

Girth strap

Ten-year-old Irish donkey, at 117 cm (11.2 hh/ 46 in)

DONKEYS OF IRELAND
Donkeys are the traditional pack and haulage animals of Ireland, which is one of the few countries in northern Europe where they have been bred for hundreds of years and where they have become adapted to a climate that is very different from the deserts where they evolved.
Irish donkeys have much shorter legs than the donkeys from the hotter Mediterranean and Arabian regions, and they have much thicker coats so they can survive the cold.

Long ears

Long tail, with tuft at tip

Well-trimmed hooves

REGAL WHITE DONKEYS
Donkeys are now popular as pets on farm parks and for children. This has led to breeding for new looks, like these white donkeys with curly coats. In the ancient world white donkeys were the favoured mounts of royalty.

Mules and hinnies

Breast collar
(easier to fit than
larger collar, as
chest is so
narrow)

Long, ass-like ears
of its father

THE SUMERIANS OF MESOPOTAMIA were the first people to interbreed horses and donkeys to produce mules (donkey father, horse mother) and hinnies (horse father, donkey mother) about 4,000 years ago. Roman writers on agriculture told how donkey stallions kept for mule-breeding were brought up with horses so that they would mate more readily with the mares. For thousands of years mules have been used as pack animals (pp.46–47) to carry huge loads, because they combine the donkey's stamina with the horse's strength. Like its parents, a mule is a herd animal that travels best in a "mule train" (a long line of mules harnessed together to pull loads). A "bell mare" (a specially trained female horse with a bell round her neck) would lead the mules who learned to follow the bell's sound, so they could travel at night without being lost in the dark. The horse family is unusual in that all the species can interbreed. Although the resulting offspring will grow to be healthy animals, they are usually sterile.

During a hard day's travel, a working mule feeds from a nose-bag filled with oats

ANCIENT EGYPTIAN EQUIDS
This ancient Egyptian tomb painting (c. 1400 BCE) shows a pair of horses drawing a chariot, while below two white hinnies are also pulling one. Their smaller ears show they are hinnies, not mules, and the straight neck, dark cross on the shoulders, and tufted tail prove they are not horses.

Crate of ducks

Large wheel makes it easier for donkey to pull this load

INDIAN TRAVEL
Mule carts are still used in Asia and have remained unchanged for at least 3,000 years. However, the method of harnessing has changed, for the earliest carts were always attached by means of a central wooden pole to a pair of mules, or horses. The idea of putting a single animal between two wooden shafts was not invented until 2,000 years ago. Here, the mule has a bridle with a bit and is driven with reins. All the family's goods are piled into the cart, including their ducks.

14-year-old mule, 140 cm (13.3 hh/ 55 in), drawing Indian cart (c. 1840)

TOURIST CLASS
People will always enjoy a leisurely drive
in a carriage and even in the busy streets
of today's large cities this is still possible.
This mule, hitched to a post decorated
with a horse's head, waits patiently to take
tourists around New Orleans, USA.

A POWERFUL MULE
Mules travelled faster than oxen and were
more sure-footed than horses over difficult
terrain, so 19th-century settlers preferred
these animals for hauling huge loads over
very bad muddy roads on their long trek
west across North America (pp.34–35).
Mules were also used as pack animals in
wartime and underground in mines.

Large body

*Heavy
head with
long ears*

*Neat
front legs*

*Strong
hind legs*

*Long tail,
like a horse*

*No forelock,
like a donkey
(pp.24–25)*

*Short
ears*

*Typical short
donkey-like
mane*

Cross-breeding

When a donkey is crossed with a horse, the foal
has what is called "hybrid vigour" – that is, it is
stronger and healthier than either of its parents.
The most common cross-breed is a donkey
stallion (or jack-ass) with a horse mare which
produces a "mule", but if a horse stallion is
crossed with a female donkey (or jenny)
the hybrid offspring is called a "hinny"
(or jennet). Generally, a mule is a
stronger animal than a hinny.

STUBBORN AS A HINNY
This eight-year old white hinny
(whose parents were a female
donkey and a pony stallion) will
not be pulled where it does not
want to go. Donkeys (pp.24–25),
mules, and hinnies all have a
reputation for being stubborn,
but this is because their natural
behavioural patterns are not
understood correctly. They are
herd animals, they are intelligent,
and they are nervous of going
to a new place on their own.
Once they are trained to follow a
person, or a bell-mare, they will
go anywhere, even to places of
great danger.

*Dark grey
spots on white,
short-haired coat*

Mule misbehaves
(pp.12–13)

*Long,
tufted
tail,
used for
swishing
flies, or to
show it is
anxious*

Eight-year-
old hinny

Old horseshoe and nails just removed from horse's hoof by farrier

Shoes and shoeing

THE HOOVES OF ALL EQUIDS are made from "keratin", a protein that is the same organic substance as hair or human finger nails. Just like hair, the hooves can be cut and shaped without discomfort to the animal. The hooves of a domestic horse wear down evenly if it is ridden over flat, hard ground, but if the land is stony the hooves will split and break. If the ground is muddy and soft, the hooves will grow too long and become diseased. It is necessary, therefore, for the horse to have regular attention from a "farrier", a person specially trained to look after hooves and fit them with metal shoes for protection. The hoof is made up of three parts – the "wall" or outer part to which the shoe is attached with nails, the "sole", and the wedge-shaped part underneath, which is called the "frog".

1 REMOVE OLD SHOE
The horse stands patiently while the farrier carefully levers off the worn old shoe.

INDIAN SHOES
The methods of shoeing horses have been much the same all over the world for hundreds of years. Here, three workers, surrounded by all their equipment, are shoeing a fine horse during the time of the Moghul emperors in northern India, c. 1600 CE.

Girth's powerful muscles enable horse to do very heavy work (pp.50–53)

Feathering on foot

Farrier's box of essential tools for shoeing horses

Shoeing a four-year-old Shire horse

GAME OF LUCK
All over the world, the horseshoe is a talisman for good luck. It must always be held with the open part at the top, so that the good luck will not drop out. Horseshoe pitching – a game based on luck – is a popular pastime in the USA and Canada. Shown here is an iron horseshoe (c. first century CE), found in southern England.

"Horn", or horseshoe-shaped excess hoof growth, removed by farrier along with old shoe

2 CLEANING THE HOOF
The excess hoof is clipped and the hoof is filed to give the correct shape for a new shoe. The whole hoof is cleaned and made ready for the new shoe.

3 AT THE FORGE
Before the farrier fits the shoe, he makes a new iron shoe at the forge. Using a heavy hammer, the farrier shapes the shoe on an anvil and then punches holes in it for the nails.

4 STEAMING
At the stables, the shoe is reheated, pressed onto the hoof to check the fit, and then allowed to cool down. The hoof gives off a smell of burning hair and much smoke, but this does not hurt the horse.

Height at withers 178 cm (17.2 hh/ 70 in)

Chestnut

6 FINISHED FOOT
The rim of the foot is then filed and so is the hoof just under the nail ends, before the farrier hammers them flat. The nails should be flush with the shoe, and the hoof and the outside edge of the shoe should match precisely.

Balancing on one front foot

Filing hoof and nail ends flat

5 NAILING ON THE SHOE
Then the farrier takes some special iron nails and hammers them through the pre-drilled holes in the shoe. The nail ends that show through the horse's hoof are wrung off and turned back.

WHEN "HIPPO" MEANT "HORSE"
Iron horseshoes were invented after the Roman period, but the Romans often tied a shoe made of wicker or metal onto the hoof with leather straps. This was called a "hipposandal", from the Greek *hippo*, meaning "horse".

Hipposandal, French, first-third century CE.

Bits and pieces

THE EARLIEST DOMESTIC horses and asses were probably ridden bareback and guided by a rope that was tied around the lower jaw in the gap between the cheek teeth and the incisors. Today this still remains a common way of controlling donkeys in Turkey and Greece. The first bits, or bridles' mouthpieces with fastenings at each end to which reins are attached, were made of hide, bone, or wood. From c. 1500 BCE bronze replaced these materials and later iron. Until late Roman times, no horseman rode with a saddle (only bareback, or on a horse cloth) and there were no stirrups (loops suspended from a horse's saddle to support the rider's foot) in Europe until the eighth century CE. The lack of saddles and stirrups did not prevent either Eurasian horsemen, or later, native Americans (pp.56–57), from holding their bows and shooting arrows from a galloping horse. The most powerful nomadic horsemen in the ancient world were the Scythians (pp.32–33) from Central Asia in the fifth and fourth centuries BCE. They had very elaborate harness, but they still rode only with a single saddle-cloth and no stirrups. These horses were the riders' most valuable possessions and were buried with them in their tombs.

Back view of woman riding sidesaddle

JINGLE BELLS
Bells on the harness were a safety feature. If horses and passengers became lost in snowbound countryside, the bells' chimes would let rescuers know their position.

SPURRED ON
The horses of the Middle Ages in 13th-century Europe had a very hard time, for they were bridled with bits and goaded by armoured knights wearing cruel spurs (U-shaped devices attached to heel of rider's boot, pp.44–45). These were either prick spurs, or rowel spurs with little wheels.

Rowel spur (length 23 cm/9 in), made of iron and brass, western European, early 1500s

Rowel

Screw would have clamped stirrup to outside of shoe

Metal part of stirrup would have fitted inside heel of shoe

Tiny rowel spur (length 4 cm/1.5 in), made of iron and fitting directly onto shoe, European, late 1600s

Buckle for attaching stirrup to boot

Metal part of stirrup for "pricking" horse

Prick spur (total length 29 cm/11 in), made of iron, Moorish, early 1800s

PUTTING YOUR FOOT IN IT
It is thought that the Chinese invented metal foot stirrups in the fifth century CE. Stirrups then spread slowly westwards to Europe. The use of stirrups altered the way in which battles were fought (pp.44–45), because they allowed horsemen to wield their weapons without falling off.

Brass fretwork

Dragon decoration

Iron stirrup, Bulgar, 800–900 CE.

Decorated boot stirrup, made of iron, Spanish, 1600s

Box stirrup, made of painted wood and brass fretwork, French or Italian, late 1700s

Brass stirrup, decorated with two dragons, Chinese, 1800s

Jointed snaffle bit,
Irish, 100 BCE–100 CE

BUILD A BETTER BIT

Three types of bit have been invented for controlling domesticated horses. The first is the simple "snaffle" bit, which developed into a jointed mouthpiece in Assyria, c. 900 BCE. A "curb" bit is unjointed with a chain running under the horse's chin, which applies pressure when the reins are used. The third bit is a "pelham", which combines the two bits of a double bridle into one. It has a curb chain and can be used with one or two reins.

joint
Rein ring

Detail from the Bayeux tapestry from France, c. 1080

DEFEAT IN BATTLE

In the Battle of Hastings, 1066, the 7,000 troops brought over from Normandy by William the Conqueror fought against the English. One reason why they won the battle was that they fought on horseback with the new invention of stirrups, while the English dismounted and fought in the old way on foot.

joint
Rein ring
Cheekpiece

Jointed snaffle bit with cheekpiece, Bulgar, 800–900 CE

Curb chain
Brass boss
Double rollers in horse's mouth
Rein ring

Curb bit (length 305 mm/12 in, width 50 mm/ 2 in), made of steel and brass, European, 1500s

Brass toss
Curb chain
Rein ring
Mouthpiece

Curb bit (length 185 mm/7 in, width 110 mm/4 in), made of steel and brass, Portuguese, 1800s

Brow band
Headpiece
Throatlatch

Height at withers 173 cm (17 hh/68 in)

Rein
Bit

RIDING SIDE-SADDLE

This grey Lipizzaner gelding is being ridden side-saddle. Women today usually only ride like this in the show ring or out hunting. In former times, from the early 1300s onwards, the side-saddle was the only way a female rider, wearing long, heavy skirts, could be mounted on a horse.

Girth
Safety stirrup
Rider on leather saddle made-to-measure in 1890

Woman, in Victorian dress, riding side-saddle on a six-year-old Lipizzaner

Rein ring (terret), English, first century CE

Strap-union made of bronze (for joining straps together), English, first century CE

Decorated terret (a ring on saddle harness through which driving reins pass), found in Egypt, first century BCE

Exploring by horse

VIKING CHESSMAN
This knight on horseback, carved from a walrus tusk during the 12th century, is one of the famous chessmen found on the Isle of Lewis off Scotland's west coast.

WITHOUT THE HORSE AND THE ASS, human history would have been quite different. Civilizations would have evolved in their places of origin and their peoples would not have travelled around the world in quest of new places to explore and conquer. There would have been no Crusades and Europeans could not have destroyed the indigenous cultures of the Americas. An invading force has to have fast transport and efficient movement of goods, weapons, and food, otherwise it is powerless against the defences of settled communities. Although horseriding was the general means of transport from at least 1,000 BCE, it was not until 2,000 years later, in the 11th century CE, that horses were commonly shod, and a saddle and stirrups generally used. From this time onwards, the horse became increasingly important in war and sport (pp.42–45), and great travellers like Marco Polo could ride huge distances across Europe and Asia – journeys that today would be considered long, even by aeroplane.

GENGHIS KHAN
Genghis Khan (1162–1227 CE), the Mongolian conqueror, ruled an empire of nomadic horsemen that stretched across Asia into Europe – from the Pacific Ocean to the Mediterranean Sea.

Pair of bronze Etruscan riders, c. 500 BCE

Statue of Charlemagne, the Holy Roman Emperor

ARCHERS OF THE ANCIENT WORLD
These two elegant Etruscan bronzes from northern Italy, c. 500 BCE, show how – even without saddle and stirrups – Scythian archers could shoot their arrows from a galloping horse. The archer shooting backwards exemplifies the "Parthian shot", a technique commonly used by the nomadic horsemen on the steppes of central Asia.

HOLY ROMAN EMPEROR
Charlemagne, or Charles the Great (742–814 CE), was the most famous ruler of the Middle Ages. As emperor of the Frankish kingdom, he conquered Saxony and Lombardy. In 796 CE, he led over 15,000 horsemen against the Avars in Hungary. In 800 CE, he was crowned Emperor of the Holy Roman Empire, stretching from Denmark to central Italy, and from France to Austria.

Fretwork

IN THE SADDLE
This 18th-century Tibetan wooden saddle, decorated with gold and silver fretwork, may have been similar to one owned by Genghis Khan 600 years earlier.

Cantle

Tree

Pommel

18th-century Tibetan saddle

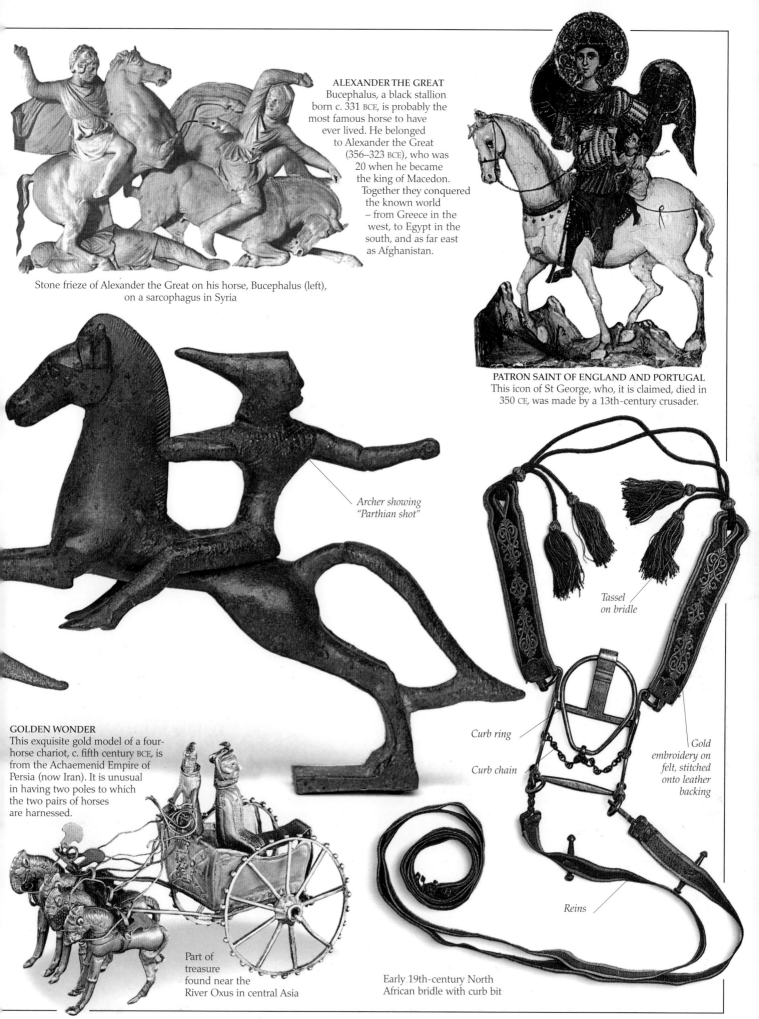

ALEXANDER THE GREAT
Bucephalus, a black stallion born c. 331 BCE, is probably the most famous horse to have ever lived. He belonged to Alexander the Great (356–323 BCE), who was 20 when he became the king of Macedon. Together they conquered the known world – from Greece in the west, to Egypt in the south, and as far east as Afghanistan.

Stone frieze of Alexander the Great on his horse, Bucephalus (left), on a sarcophagus in Syria

PATRON SAINT OF ENGLAND AND PORTUGAL
This icon of St George, who, it is claimed, died in 350 CE, was made by a 13th-century crusader.

Archer showing "Parthian shot"

GOLDEN WONDER
This exquisite gold model of a four-horse chariot, c. fifth century BCE, is from the Achaemenid Empire of Persia (now Iran). It is unusual in having two poles to which the two pairs of horses are harnessed.

Part of treasure found near the River Oxus in central Asia

Tassel on bridle

Curb ring

Curb chain

Gold embroidery on felt, stitched onto leather backing

Reins

Early 19th-century North African bridle with curb bit

To the Americas

FINE HATS
For ceremonial occasions the Sioux Chieftains, from America's northern plains, wear their finest headdresses, made of wild turkey feathers, and ride their most beautiful horses.

BEFORE 1492 when the first European settlers arrived in both North and South America, the continents were densely populated with the native peoples, who had arrived there between 20,000 and 10,000 years earlier. The European invaders had a fast means of transport – the horse and the mule – so they were able to conquer the native Americans and take over vast areas of land. Soon a few horses escaped to live and breed in the wild. Within a hundred years they had spread over all the grasslands (pp.36–37). The native Americans of both continents soon realized the value of the horse. By bartering with the Spanish, they obtained their own stock which they learned to ride with as much dexterity as the ancient Scythians (pp.32–33), who could shoot an arrow from a bow while riding a galloping horse without stirrups.

THE BLACK HAWK WAR
Like other North American tribes, the Sauk Indians of the northern Mississippi River prized their horses, using them for transport, hunting, and in war. Keokuk (above, c. 1760–1848), who had been appointed Sauk chief by US officials, signed treaties giving away much of the Sauk land. Black Hawk, the Sauks' true leader, and his people fiercely defended their land, but were defeated in the end. By 1840 millions of acres of Indian territory were ceded to the whites.

BEASTS OF BURDEN
Before there were railways across the North American continent, teams of six or more mules (pp.26–27) would haul heavily-laden waggons along roads that were often deep in mud and impassable by any other means of transport.

Blaze

Central wooden shaft, or "tongue", to which harness is attached

Martingale

Stocking

DOWN MEXICO WAY
In the early 1500s, Spanish conquistadors brought horses (similar to Andalusians, pp.40–41) to the New World, where they had been extinct for 10,000 years. Here Indians present Hernando Cortés (1485–1547), the conqueror of Mexico, with a treasured necklace.

Shod hoof giving better grip in soft earth

WESTWARD HO!

Trappers, traders, and missionaries were the first to reach the Pacific, but in 1843 a determined band of 1,000 settlers left Missouri on the 3,300-km (2,000-mile) trek westwards along the Oregon Trail. To protect themselves from attack, they would form their waggons into a circle at dusk. Finally after many gruelling months, bad weather, disease, poor food, and crossing the Rocky Mountains, they reached their destination.

Canvas held up by iron hoop underneath

Waterproofed heavy-duty canvas top

Brake lever

Whippletree, attaching harness to waggon

Trace

Pair of Gelderlanders (168 cm/16.2 hh/66 in) pulling "prairie schooner"

Axle supporting massive weight of waggon and its load

Iron rim over wooden wheel

Metal hub

AMERICA'S FIRST MOBILE HOME

The early European settlers travelled across North America with their children and all their belongings in a covered waggon, or "prairie schooner". It was a hard life for they had to be entirely self-sufficient, knowing how to shoe a horse (pp.28–29), mend a wheel, bake bread, and nurse the sick.

Front wheel, 123 cm (4 ft) across, is smaller to allow sharp turning

SOUTHERN COWBOY

The horsemen, or gauchos, of the South American pampas work mainly on huge ranches. Like the cowboys of North America, they spend their lives in the saddle, expertly rounding up cattle.

Running wild

THERE ARE NO LONGER ANY TRULY WILD HORSES living in the wild, but all over the world there are many herds of horses and ponies that are described as "feral". Feral animals are descended from domesticated stock but are no longer under human control and they live and breed in the wild. The last truly wild horses were the Przewalski's horses (pp.20–21) that survived in small numbers on the Mongolian steppes until the 1960s. In North and South America, horses spread very rapidly over the grasslands soon after the first Europeans arrived (pp.34–35), at the end of the 15th century, bringing their horses and donkeys with them. Soon there were large herds of horses and donkeys living wild in the grasslands and deserts. In western USA, these horses are known as mustangs and the donkeys as burros. Similar feral horses in Australia are called brumbies. Today their numbers are controlled and some are domesticated.

Long ears

FELL PONIES
In Britain there are many breeds of pony that live on the moors, like the Fell pony. Although Fell ponies are owned, they are allowed to live and breed with very little human control. Traditionally, the Fell ponies have been used as pack ponies, for riding, and for light draught work.

Well-proportioned head

Coat colours vary from bay, brown, and grey, but never piebald or skewbald (pp.38–41)

GERMAN DÜLMEN
These rare ponies live semi-wild on the Duke of Croy's estate in Westphalia in Germany. They have been cross-bred with both British and Polish ponies, so they are not pure-bred. The herd dates back to the early 1300s.

Strong legs support sturdy, well-built body

THE BRUMBY OF AUSTRALIA
For 150 years there have been herds of feral horses in Australia, ever since they were abandoned during the gold rush. These horses, called brumbies, formed herds and reproduced in great numbers over large areas. They are unpopular with cattle and sheep ranchers because they compete for grazing, and usually carry many parasites. Since the 1960s, they have been hunted so extensively that there are now very few.

Well-formed feet with strong horn

SYMBOLIC HORSES
A wild running horse has often been used as a symbol of freedom and elegance. It has advertised many things, from banks to sports cars – such as the Mustang and Pinto in the USA, and (as shown here) the Ferrari, the supreme speedster.

THE MUSTANGS OF AMERICA
The feral horses, or mustangs, of the Nevada desert in the USA have hard lives travelling great distances in search of enough grass and water to live on.

DAWN IN THE CAMARGUE
The beautiful white horses from the Camargue in the south of France have lived wild in the marshes of the Rhône delta for over a thousand years. They have very wide hooves for living on soft wet grassland.

Short stripe on face

Star

Long, straight, full mane

Snip

Deep girth

Full forelock

New Forest ponies range in height from 127–147 cm (12.2 to l4.2 hh/50–58 in)

Blaze

THE PONIES OF THE NEW FOREST
In Britain there have been herds of ponies living in the New Forest woodlands of Hampshire, England since the 11th century. For 800 years these ponies lived wild there, but in the 19th century attempts were made to improve them by bringing in stallions of other breeds. They still run wild in their native area, but also are reared on private stud farms and provide ideal riding ponies for children and adults, and for light draught work (pp.54–55).

Horses from around the world

THE DIFFERENT BREEDS OF HORSE are often divided by breeders into three types. First are "hotbloods", or "fullbloods" – the Arab and Thoroughbred breeds. These horses have the same blood temperature as other breeds so they really do not have "hot blood", but are given this name because they are descended from the Arab and Barb breeds from the hot countries of North Africa and Arabia. Second are "coldbloods", which again do not have cold blood, but they are the large, heavy draught horses (pp.50–53) from cold, northern climates. Third are "warm-bloods", or "halfbreds", which are crosses between hotbloods and coldbloods. It is this group that supplies most modern sporting horses (pp.59–61), except for the racehorses which are almost always Thoroughbreds. All Thoroughbreds can trace their ancestry back to three famous stallions – the Byerly Turk (c. 1689), the Darley Arabian (c. 1702), and the Godolphin Arabian (c. 1731).

Grey coat is black skin, with a mixture of white and black hairs, as in this Connemara pony from Ireland

Dapple-grey occurs when dark grey hairs form rings on a grey coat, as in this Orlov Trotter from Russia

Palomino (a colour, not a breed) is a gold coat, with white mane and tail, and very little black, as in this Haflinger pony from Austria

Chestnut occurs in various shades of gold – from pale gold to a rich, red gold, as in this French Trotter from Normandy in France

Bay is a reddish coat, with black mane, tail, and "points" (ears, legs, and muzzle), as in this Cleveland Bay from England

Coronet is the white hair just above the hoof

Sock is the white hair reaching halfway up the cannon bone

Stocking is the white hair reaching up to the knee, or the hock (pp.10–11)

Brown is mixed black and brown in coat, with brown mane, tail, and legs, as in this Nonius from Hungary

Decorated bridle

Height at withers 150 cm (14.3 hh/ 59 in)

Four-year-old, pure-bred Arab, mahogany bay in colour

BARBS AND BERBERS
The Barb, second only to the Arab as the world's first horse breed, has long been the traditional mount of North African tribesmen (Berbers). Here, Moroccan horsemen display their riding skills at a festival.

REARING UP
Because horses are so beautiful and can be trained so easily, they are indispensible for circus entertainment. They seem to enjoy carrying out difficult and unusual movements with their bodies, as shown here.

Height at withers 145 cm (14.1 hh/57 in)

COATS OF MANY COLOURS
In this elaborate painting, made by Indian artists from the Mughal school (c. 1590), a crow is addressing an assembly of animals in this Persian fable. They include several horses in a variety of coat colours – chestnut, light and dappled greys, bay, and skewbald (pp.40–41).

15-year-old Arab, very light grey colour with tiny dapples in coat

HORSE FAIR
For many centuries, horses have been bought and sold at horse sales around the world, as shown in this detail of a painting by English artist, John Herring (1795–1865).

ARISTOCRATIC ARAB
The Arab is the aristocrat of horses with its elegant head, slender limbs, high carriage of the tail, and fiery temperament. Arabs have been carefully bred and records kept of their pedigrees for perhaps a thousand years in their countries of origin in North Africa and Arabia.

Embroidered saddle-cloth

Other breeds and colours

EVERY COUNTRY HAS ITS OWN BREED OF HORSE – from India's polo pony to southern Africa's Basuto pony, and Britain's Shire horse (pp.50–53). Each breed is adapted to life in its place of origin and each has its own uses. The breeds are defined by their "conformation", or size and body shape, as well as by their colour and any white markings they may have on their faces and legs. Horses come in many different sizes – from the smallest horse in the world, the Falabella which measures no more than 76 cm (7.2 hh/30 in) at the withers, to the largest of all breeds, the Shire horse. A Shire stallion should be 168 cm (16.2 hh/66 in) or above, and should weigh about one tonne (one ton). Shires are usually black or bay with a white blaze on their forehead, or grey. Their heavily feathered feet have white socks or stockings (pp.38–39). There are many sayings linking horses' behaviour with their coat colours. There is an Arab saying that all horses but bays are unlucky, unless they have white markings, and another that a white horse is the most princely but that it suffers from the heat. There is a widespread belief too that chestnuts are fast but hot-tempered.

Height at withers 165 cm (16.1 hh/65 in)

Flat metal stirrup

STARS ...
It is usual for horses to have white markings on their faces, such as a regular, or irregular, "star" shape set high on the face between the eyes. An example is this Danish Warmblood, a breed now regarded as Denmark's national horse. A small white patch between the nostrils is called a "snip".

... AND STRIPES
A long, narrow strip of white, extending from above the eyes to the nostrils, is called a "stripe", as on this Oldenburg, a breed first established in Germany in the 1600s. A stripe can also be "interrupted", with the coat colour showing between the star, short stripe, and snip down the horse's face.

WHAT THE BLAZES!
A wide strip starting above the eyes extending down to the muzzle is called a "blaze", as on this Gelderlander from the Netherlands, a breed which has existed for the last century. When white hair covers almost all the face from the forelock to the lips, this is called a "white face".

Seven-year-old, dark grey, pure-bred Andalusian ridden by a woman in classical Spanish riding costume

CLASSICAL EQUITATION
The Spanish Riding School was founded in 1572, when nine Lipizzaner stallions and 24 mares were brought to Vienna in Austria from Spain.

HORSES IN ART

The beauty, elegance, and strength of the horse has fascinated sculptors and artists for thousands of years (pp.22–23, 32–33). In this stylized work by the German painter, Franz Marc (1880–1916), these horses have a symbolic blue colour to their coats.

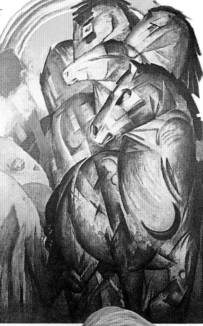

THE "SPANISH HORSE"

Known as the "Spanish Horse" for centuries, Andalusian horses were first bred by Carthusian monks at three monasteries in southwest Spain at the end of the 1400s. The breed was influenced possibly by the Barbs of North Africa (pp.38–39). Today the horses are usually bay or grey, but they were originally chestnut or black.

Numnah (sheepskin pad to protect horse's back)

Spanish-style saddle blanket

Exhibiting spectacular passage, a slow-tempo trot with exaggerated elevation of legs

Horses are called black when the coat, mane, tail, and legs are completely black, as in this beautiful Friesian from the Netherlands.

Roan colour can be either "strawberry" (where the coat colour is chestnut with white hairs mixed), or "blue" (a black or brown coat with a percentage of white hair), as in this Italian Heavy Draught horse from Venice in northern Italy

Dun colour can be a blue, mouse, or light yellow coat (with black in the legs, mane, and tail), as in this Fjord pony from Norway. The "dorsal eel stripe" running along the mane and back into the tail is typical of this breed

A spotted coat can have five varieties of pattern, usually dark spots on light hair, as seen here in this minute Falabella, first bred in Argentina

Skewbald refers to large, white patches on another coat colour. This Pinto pony from the USA has a chestnut coat with white patches (called "Ovaro"), but a white coat with coloured patches is called "Tobiano"

Usually piebald means large, irregular patches of white and black hairs in the coat, as in this Shetland pony from the Scottish islands of the same name

War horses

THE HORSE AND THE ASS have been used by people to assist them in their wars of invasion for the last 5,000 years. By riding in chariots harnessed to a pair of asses, or horses, men could travel much faster than on foot and could cause much greater damage to the enemy. At first there were small squabbles between individuals, but then families grew larger and settled into villages, and battles took place between the men. When armed horseriders (or cavalry) were developed from the time of Alexander the Great (pp.32–33), the horse played a major role in all wars until just after World War I, when mechanized vehicles took over. After stirrups became wide-spread in Europe in the early Medieval period (pp.30–31), the cavalry was more protected from attack by riding new, higher saddles (with stirrups) that gave a steadier seat, and was able to use longer weapons, like lances. This meant that armour had to be heavier and larger horses had to be bred, but they were never as large as the heavy horses of today.

NAPOLEON'S FAVOURITE CHARGER
Marengo was the white Arab pony ridden by the French leader, Napoleon Bonaparte (1769–1821), during the Battle of Waterloo in Belgium in 1815 when he was defeated by the British. Although wounded during this battle, Marengo did not die until 1829.

Rider's uniform heavily embroidered with real gold thread

Made of pure silver, these drums weigh 68 kg (150 lb)

Royal coat of arms (featuring a lion and a unicorn) embroidered with real gold and silver threads on damask silk of drum banner

Bridle's beard, or tussle, made of natural horse hair – black hair surrounding dyed red hair

Double reins covered with real gold thread – boot reins connected to rider's stirrups, second set to rider's waist

TILTING AT WINDMILLS
In 1605, the Spanish poet, Miguel Cervantes (1547–1616) created his most memorable character, Don Quixote, and his mare, Rosinante. He and his friend Sancho Panza (who rode a donkey) had all kinds of adventures, but their most famous one occurred when they used their lances to attack "giants" – which were really windmills.

THE DRUM HORSE OF THE HOUSEHOLD CAVALRY
Today the drum horse is only used during processions, but before the time of the tank and the aeroplane, the beating of drums and the blowing of trumpets were always to give men courage as they were led into battle. These drums were presented by King William IV of England to the Life Guards regiment of his Household Cavalry in 1830.

Fifteen-year-old, blue roan Clydesdale carrying two pure silver drums and rider, from the Household Cavalry of Queen Elizabeth II of Great Britain and the Commonwealth

Red Cross flag

The first ambulances, like this World War I example, were harnessed to a pair of horses or mules

Whippletree to which horse's harness was hitched to vehicle

Brake

Small front wheel to allow sharp turning

Large rear wheel to carry heavy loads

INTO BATTLE

The Charge of the Light Brigade – resulting in huge casualties of both horses and men – was the most disastrous battle of the Crimean War (1853–1856), fought between Russia on one side and Britain, Turkey, France, and Sardinia on the other. The Crimea is a small area of land to the north of the Black Sea in the Ukraine.

TIBETAN WARRIOR

For hundreds of years, the Tibetan cavalry used a form of armour made of small metal plates ("lamellae") laced together with leather thongs. This type of armour, for both horse and rider, had been used by the nomadic warriors of central Asia and was very similar to that worn by the Mongols when they overran Asia and Eastern Europe (pp.32–33). The Tibetans have preserved this traditional armour – even into the 20th century.

Metal shaffron for protecting horse's head

Crinet for protecting horse's neck

Peytral to protect horse's breast

Leather lace

Small metal plate

Crupper protecting horse's hind quarters

Tibetan cavalry armour, for horse and rider, used between the 17th and 19th centuries

AUSTRALIAN ARTILLERY

The Waler (named after New South Wales in Australia where horses were first imported 200 years ago) was the world's finest cavalry horse during World War I. These horses were strong and hardy, able to carry heavy loads, had good stamina and an amiable temperament. Now the Australian Stock Horse, based on the Waler, is used widely on cattle stations for herding.

Nineteenth-century British cavalry spur, made of nickel silver

STURDY STIRRUPS

The stirrup was the most important innovation in the history of the horse in war, because it enabled a heavily-armed rider to stay on his horse. Shown here is an 18th-century British cavalry stirrup, made of brass.

NECESSITIES OF WAR

No battle could be fought without supplies of food, water, and arms hauled to the Front Line by pack horses and mules.

Whippletree

Tongue

Metal barrel containing water for either troops or animals

World War I water waggon, made in England, used in France, hauled by two horses

GHANAIAN WARRIOR

This brass model of a warrior on horseback was cast in Ghana in West Africa during the 18th century.

The age of chivalry

SAMURAI WARRIOR
This screen painting depicts a 12th-century Japanese samurai warrior going into battle. The honourable samurai, who wore two swords and a distinctive headdress, was totally loyal to his feudal lord.

THE POLITICS OF EUROPE WAS DOMINATED by the feudal system during the 11th and 12th centuries. Some knights were feudal lords, who owned tracts of land and granted its use to their vassals. They also owned serfs, over whom they had complete power. These knights were Christians, bound by the code of chivalry – a religious, moral, and social code that covered every aspect of their lives. The ideal knight was brave, courteous, and honourable, and totally dedicated to war against all non-Christians. By 1200, much of Europe was settled under feudalism and armed knights began the conquest of new lands in the east. The Crusades were fought over territory, but religious passion and the principles of chivalry meant that leaders, such as Richard the Lionheart, could depend on their armed knights to give up their lives for the cause of winning Jerusalem from the Muslims.

European, late 19th-century brass copy of 15th-century medieval spur with rowel (pp.30–31), which had to be long to reach under the horse's armour

Lambrequin, or mantling

Leather gauntlet, or glove

Blunted wooden lance

Cloth surcoat

Caparison, or colourful, decorated horse covering

Mail armour

THE ROMANCE OF THE JOUST
The armed knights learned how to fight on horseback in tournaments. This sport, known as "justing", or "jousting" (from the Latin *juxtare*, meaning to meet together), was part of the code of chivalry. The heavily armed knights tried to win points by either unhorsing their opponents or by breaking their own lances (up to 2.5 m/8 ft long) against the other's shields. From the dangerous hand-to-hand fighting, or mêlées, of the 12th century to the colourful pageantry of the 15th and 16th centuries, competitive tournaments were very popular spectator sports until their decline during the 17th century.

Reconstruction of a pair of sporting jousters from the early 14th century

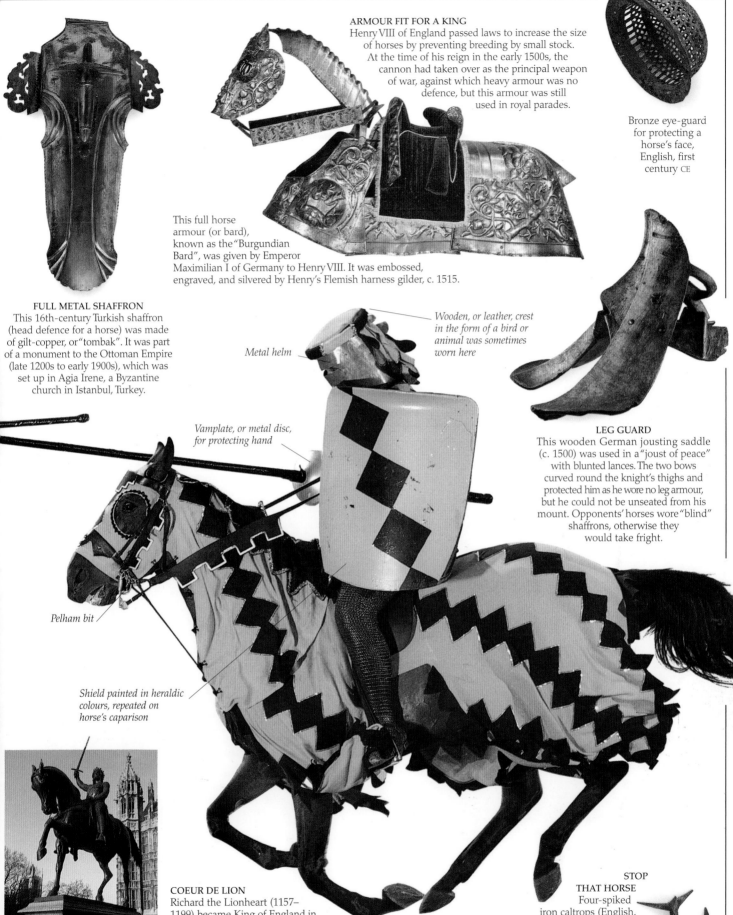

FULL METAL SHAFFRON
This 16th-century Turkish shaffron (head defence for a horse) was made of gilt-copper, or "tombak". It was part of a monument to the Ottoman Empire (late 1200s to early 1900s), which was set up in Agia Irene, a Byzantine church in Istanbul, Turkey.

ARMOUR FIT FOR A KING
Henry VIII of England passed laws to increase the size of horses by preventing breeding by small stock. At the time of his reign in the early 1500s, the cannon had taken over as the principal weapon of war, against which heavy armour was no defence, but this armour was still used in royal parades.

This full horse armour (or bard), known as the "Burgundian Bard", was given by Emperor Maximilian I of Germany to Henry VIII. It was embossed, engraved, and silvered by Henry's Flemish harness gilder, c. 1515.

Bronze eye-guard for protecting a horse's face, English, first century CE

Metal helm

Wooden, or leather, crest in the form of a bird or animal was sometimes worn here

LEG GUARD
This wooden German jousting saddle (c. 1500) was used in a "joust of peace" with blunted lances. The two bows curved round the knight's thighs and protected him as he wore no leg armour, but he could not be unseated from his mount. Opponents' horses wore "blind" shaffrons, otherwise they would take fright.

Vamplate, or metal disc, for protecting hand

Pelham bit

Shield painted in heraldic colours, repeated on horse's caparison

COEUR DE LION
Richard the Lionheart (1157–1199) became King of England in 1189. In 1190, he embarked on the Third Crusade to Palestine, where his bravery gave him immortal fame. He returned to England and spent the rest of his life warring against France.

STOP THAT HORSE
Four-spiked iron caltrops (English, first–second century CE), were placed in the ground to lame the enemy's horses when they stepped on them.

Travelling by horse

HORSES, ASSES, AND MULES have been used to transport people and their goods from place to place for more than 4,000 years. The first harness and carts had to be made entirely of wood, bone, and leather, until about 3,500 years ago when copper and bronze began to be used on chariots, followed by iron about 2,500 years ago. The use of metals for parts of the harness – like rein rings (terrets) and bits, and on carts for the rims of wheels (tyres) and for hubs and axles – greatly increased the efficiency and speed of transport, especially in southern Europe and Asia where the climate is dry. But in northern Europe, with its high rainfall, the pack horse remained the most practical means of travel (especially in winter) until roads were built, first by the Romans, and then not again until the Middle Ages (1100–1500 CE).

FIT FOR A QUEEN
This is a replica of Queen Elizabeth I's carriage – the first carriage to be built for the British monarchy. Before this time, royalty had to ride in carts. Made of wood, with steps that folded up to form part of the side, the carriage had a padded roof, which provided protection from the rain.

HIGHWAYMAN AND HORSE
Dick Turpin (1706–1739) was a legendary English highwayman who, it has been recorded, rode to the city of York in record time on his mount Black Bess.

HORSE FEATHERS
The horses of the native Americans had endless endurance and great stamina for use in both war and hunting. Colour and decoration were part of the native Americans' culture. The chiefs would wear magnificent feathered headdresses and they would adorn their horses as well.

BAREBACK RIDER!
An 11th-century legend records that Lady Godiva rode naked through Coventry in a protest against heavy taxes imposed by her husband.

Blinker

Blaze

Bit with a straight bar

Collar

Metal hame with twist at top as traditional Romany decoration

Breeching strap

BEAST OF BURDEN
This stone frieze shows that, about 2,600 years ago, the ancient Assyrians bred powerful mules (pp.26–27) to carry their hunting gear.

THE TRAVELLERS
For hundreds of years, Romany gypsies have travelled around Europe living in their caravans. No one knows where they came from, although they may be of Hindu origin. Today, people like to use these horse-drawn vehicles for holidays.

PATRON SAINT
St Christopher (third century CE) was the patron saint of travellers – his feast day is 25 July. A St Christopher's medal has always been a symbol of good luck..

18th-century bronze horse and rider from Nigeria in West Africa

PILGRIMS' PROGRESS
Pilgrims to Canterbury Cathedral were immortalized by the English poet Geoffrey Chaucer (c. 1345–1400) in his legendary *Canterbury Tales*.

Canvas-covered barrel top

Shaft

Sock

Nine-year-old Irish Draught horse (wearing traditional Romany harness) pulling a gypsy caravan, built in Ireland, c. 1850

Horse-drawn vehicles

Snow sled with fur-lined seats for passengers and driver, built in the Netherlands, c. 1880

Bronze model of horse and carriage, Eastern Han Dynasty of China, second century CE

THE EARLIEST CHARIOTS in the ancient world had solid wooden wheels and a fixed axle that did not pivot. The invention of light, spoked wheels, like those shown here, meant that the chariot, or carriage, could travel much faster. The four-wheeled carriage, with a swivelling axle that could turn independently of the body, was a further improvement which became common only in the early Middle Ages. Just as today people show their status in society by the kind of motor car they own, in the past they did the same with their horse and carriage. The poor travelled in carts and on horse buses, while the rich travelled in superb carriages harnessed to the most perfect horses. Great effort went into maintaining horses, harness, and carriages. Horses had to be fed and fitted with shoes (which is why so many people of English ancestry are called Smith), wheels had to be greased and repaired (giving another surname, Wheeler), and the carriages had to be kept clean and dry.

Elegant and expensive carriage harnessed to a pair of beautifully turned-out horses

WHOSE LAND IS IT ANYWAY?
The early European immigrants who travelled across North America by stagecoach were often attacked by mounted native Americans, armed with stolen or bartered guns, as depicted in this painting by American artist George Inness (1854–1926).

Blinker

Collar

Terret

Crupper

Check, or driving, rein

Hame

Bit

Martingale

Girth strap

Hip strap

Tongue

Trace

Triple whippletree connecting two pairs of horses to stagecoach

Only one seat left on this overcrowded horse bus – two people will be disappointed

Driver's seat

Seating for two passengers

A type of Victorian carriage called a barouche, made in England from a French design, c. 1880

WAY OUT WEST

Two American businessmen – Henry Wells (1805–1878) and William Fargo (1818–1881) – opened their offices in San Francisco in 1852 to provide banking and shipping services, linking the Far West with the rest of the nation. The famous Wells Fargo stage-coaches would carry private passengers, post, money, and other valuables.

Guard-messenger riding shotgun

"Jehu", or driver

Extra luggage stowed on top

Roll-up leather curtains to let in cool air, or to keep out snow and rain

Brake lever operated by driver's foot

WELLS FARGO & CO. OVERLAND STAGE

U.S. MAIL

Seating inside for nine passengers – three each on three benches

Passengers' luggage stowed in rear trunk

Two sets of reins connecting the two pairs to driver

Step for passengers getting into stagecoach

Box under driver's seat containing tools, water bucket, mail pouches, and strongboxes full of valuables

Two pairs of Welsh Cobs hauling Wells Fargo stagecoach, made in USA, late 1800s

Standing room for up to 12 passengers

Driver's seat

Hunting brake, with driver's seat and space for standing room only, made in England, c. 1880

49

Heavy horses

In europe and asia, "the age of the horse" lasted from the classical times of Greece and Rome until the beginning of the 19th century. During this long period, until they were overtaken by the steam engine, not only were the horse, mule, and donkey the chief means of transport, they were also totally necessary for all kinds of agricultural work. They were used for forestry, pulling brewers' drays, harvesting, and threshing on the land, as well as for drawing water from wells. In the Mediterranean and Middle East areas, where the soils are light and dry, the donkey (pp.24–25) carried out these tasks. In northern Europe, where the soils are damp and full of sticky clay, powerful heavy horses were needed for ploughing and haulage along the muddy roads. Today the heavy horses of Britain and Europe are exported around the world – to the USA and Canada, Australia, and Japan.

HAYMAKING IN IRELAND
The horse and the donkey are still used on small farms in Ireland. Here in Connemara, County Galway, a waggon is being loaded with stooks of hay, which will provide food for the farm animals during the winter.

Long, arched neck with thick mane

Fine head with straight profile

BELGIAN COMPACT
Also called Brabant, this ancient breed of magnificent heavy draught horses from Belgium has remained pure-bred. They are still used as farm horses and are particularly popular in the USA.

Decorated mane

Horse brass

Hame, on heavy collar

Broad, deep-chested body

Chestnut-coloured Belgian Draught horse

BEFORE THE TRACTOR
The invention of the rigid, padded horse collar by the Chinese, c. 500 CE, spread across Asia to Europe. The subsequent effect on agriculture was enormous and horse-drawn ploughs became the tractors of their day. Nowadays, ploughing with horses is slower than using a tractor, but some farmers find it more satisfying work and it is better for the land. Ploughing competitions still take place each year at agricultural shows in Britain, Europe, and North America, as shown by these two superb Shire horses (left).

Strong, muscular leg

No feathering on heel of foot

Dapple-grey Percheron

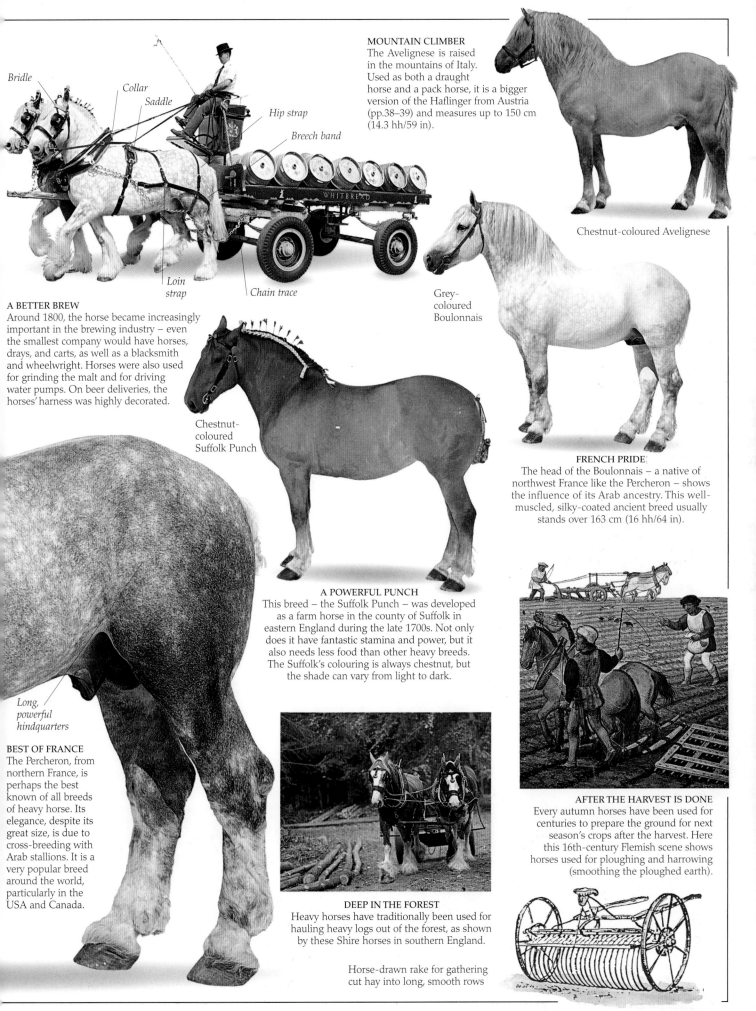

Bridle

Collar

Saddle

Hip strap

Breech band

WHITBREAD

Loin strap

Chain trace

MOUNTAIN CLIMBER
The Avelignese is raised
in the mountains of Italy.
Used as both a draught
horse and a pack horse, it is a bigger
version of the Haflinger from Austria
(pp.38–39) and measures up to 150 cm
(14.3 hh/59 in).

Chestnut-coloured Avelignese

Grey-
coloured
Boulonnais

A BETTER BREW
Around 1800, the horse became increasingly
important in the brewing industry – even
the smallest company would have horses,
drays, and carts, as well as a blacksmith
and wheelwright. Horses were also used
for grinding the malt and for driving
water pumps. On beer deliveries, the
horses' harness was highly decorated.

Chestnut-
coloured
Suffolk Punch

FRENCH PRIDE
The head of the Boulonnais – a native of
northwest France like the Percheron – shows
the influence of its Arab ancestry. This well-
muscled, silky-coated ancient breed usually
stands over 163 cm (16 hh/64 in).

A POWERFUL PUNCH
This breed – the Suffolk Punch – was developed
as a farm horse in the county of Suffolk in
eastern England during the late 1700s. Not only
does it have fantastic stamina and power, but it
also needs less food than other heavy breeds.
The Suffolk's colouring is always chestnut, but
the shade can vary from light to dark.

*Long,
powerful
hindquarters*

BEST OF FRANCE
The Percheron, from
northern France, is
perhaps the best
known of all breeds
of heavy horse. Its
elegance, despite its
great size, is due to
cross-breeding with
Arab stallions. It is a
very popular breed
around the world,
particularly in the
USA and Canada.

AFTER THE HARVEST IS DONE
Every autumn horses have been used for
centuries to prepare the ground for next
season's crops after the harvest. Here
this 16th-century Flemish scene shows
horses used for ploughing and harrowing
(smoothing the ploughed earth).

DEEP IN THE FOREST
Heavy horses have traditionally been used for
hauling heavy logs out of the forest, as shown
by these Shire horses in southern England.

Horse-drawn rake for gathering
cut hay into long, smooth rows

Horse power

WITHOUT THE HORSE, the industrial revolution at the end of the 18th century could never have taken place. Horse transport enabled manufactured goods to be carried to ships for export to foreign countries and it enabled people to flock to the cities for work in the new industries. Horses were used in the factories to provide power to engines and machines for grinding malt for brewing (pp.50–51) or wheat for flour, spinning cotton, and furnace blowing. In the mines, ponies were used underground for hauling loads from the coal face (pp.62–63) and above ground for towing barges full of coal along the canals. Horses also hauled buses, fire engines, and goods waggons. Today, there are few places where the horse has not been replaced by machinery, but the term used to measure the pulling power of an engine is still "horsepower". One horsepower is equivalent to 746 watts and one metric horsepower equals 736 watts.

Cog

Shaft attached to grinding stones

HORSE BUSES
The first public horse carriages in Britain started in 1564, but the roads were so bad that people could not travel far, especially in winter.

Weighing scales

COAL MERCHANT
THOMAS JEWELL

Heavily laden coal waggon, made in England, 1920

Sack of coal

Brake

SNOWSHOES
In heavy snow, a sturdy team of surefooted horses is needed to haul logs out of forests, or sleds full of people or goods, as shown by these Haflinger ponies in Bavaria in southern Germany.

Lamp

Horn

Water hose

LONDON

Water bucket

EXPLORING THE INTERIOR
Teams of horses hauled wooden waggons laden with supplies to Australia's interior, such as this area of New South Wales. The safety of these waggons depended upon the wheels being made correctly.

Victorian fire engine, English, 1890 – wheels were wide to allow horses to turn sharply around corners without risking a spill

Giant iron fly-wheel attached to an iron rod, or shaft

GOING ROUND IN CIRCLES
The tediousness of this circular work is all the more apparent when viewed from above.

Heavy collar

Whippletree attached to iron bar, in turn linked to shaft

Metal linked-chain trace

Long, well-muscled leg helping horse pull heavy load

Huge, flat grinding stones hidden underground

Shire horse pulling heavy horse gin, or horsewheel, inside a circular building called a roundhouse

TOWING A BARGE
Horses and mules were often used to pull barges heavily laden with coal or farm produce along rivers and canals in Britain and Europe – an efficient means of transport that lasted well into the 20th century.

A HARD GRIND
This horse is being used to turn a mill wheel to grind corn into flour – just as horses, mules (pp.26–27), and donkeys (pp.24–25) have done all over Europe since Roman times. The animals were forced to walk round and round in a small circle for hours on end, pulling the rope or chain that turned the heavy grinding stone. Sometimes, a pair of horses would carry out this operation – they had to be specially trained to keep to a steady pace and at the correct speed.

Light draught work

THEY MAY NOT BE AS ELEGANT as the Thoroughbred, or as magnificent as the heavy horse, but the common light draught horses were the mainstay of transport throughout the world until the invention of the steam engine in the 1820s. Light draught horses pulled every kind of waggon, carriage, and cart. These horses had to be powerful and fast, as well as able to cover long distances without becoming tired. Normally, they did not belong to any particular breed but some – like the Cleveland Bay of Yorkshire in northern England – had been preserved as pure breeds since ancient times. Originally, Cleveland Bays were known as "Chapman horses" because they were used to carry the loads of travelling salesmen, or "chapmen", around the countryside.

Hansom cab (c. 1850), designed for two passengers, driven by single driver and horse

CROWD CONTROL
The specially trained horses of mounted police still perform an important function in being able to move fast through crowds of people. They provide their riders with mobility and a good view of events.

Feathered plume

PACK HORSE
For centuries, horses have been used for carrying heavy loads on their backs. This woodcutter's horse in Guatemala is laden with planks of wood.

Pole strap attaching collar to central shaft (pole)

Royal coat of arms

Barred Victorian gaol waggon used to carry prisoners, made in England, c. 1890

Black velvet pall, or blanket, covering horse's hindquarters

DAYS OF MOURNING
In the old days, a black-draped hearse, drawn by a pair of black-plumed horses, was an impressive sight as it slowly carried the coffin to a funeral.

SUNDAY MORNING DRIVE
A family enjoys an outing in their horse-drawn carriage, in this print by American lithographers Nathaniel Currier (1813–1888) and James Ives (1824–1895).

Harness attached to centre pole

Pair of greys and phaeton, English, c. 1840

REGENCY RAKE ABOUT TOWN
In English spa towns in the early part of the 19th century, young gentlemen would dash about town driving their latest status symbol, such as this convertible model – an elegant sporting phaeton driven with the top up or down.

Driver dressed in dark mourning suit

Plumes made of ostrich feathers

Coffin

Engraved glass sides

Splinter bar to which traces are attached

Pair of black Welsh Cobs, in black and silver harness, pulling funeral hearse, made in England, c. 1850

R. JORDAN & SONS

THE PADDOCK

Rubber-wheeled dairy waggon, made in England, c. 1950

The horse in North America

THE INDIGENOUS WILD HORSES (equids) of North America became extinct about 10,000 years ago. The first domestic horses landed on the continent 9,500 years later with Christopher Columbus in 1492. Since then horses have symbolized freedom and enterprise in North America and for the next 425 years the increase in horse numbers matched that of humans. Horses have been constant companions of nearly everyone. They have drawn very heavy loads in the searing heat of deserts, down deep mines, and along muddy roads. The horse transformed the lives of native Americans who had previously hauled their possessions by dog sled and on their own backs.

With the horse, people had a new means of fast transport and also could hunt buffalo (American bison) much more efficiently.

BUFFALO BILL
In 1882, former Pony Express rider (p.62) Buffalo Bill Cody (1846–1917) put on the first professional rodeo show at the Fourth of July celebrations in Nebraska, with contests in shooting, riding, and bronco-busting.

TRAVEL TODAY
The Amish settled in Pennsylvania, USA, in the early 1700s and developed the Conestoga (a heavier version of the covered waggon) which helped explore the West (pp.34–35). Today their simple lifestyle means that they still use horses for both work and travel.

A MUSICAL RIDE
The Royal Canadian Mounted Police (founded in 1873) are world famous for the splendid pageantry – red tunics, black horses, bright banners – of their musical ride.

Stetson hat

Fringed leather jacket

Saddle horn

Stock whip

Flowing mane

Western curb bit

LEGENDARY LADIES
Calamity Jane, Annie Oakley, Belle Starr … the list of female legends of the Old West is endless, when cowgirls had to ride a horse, shoot a gun, and cope with everything as well as any man. The bad guys and girls – like Frank and Jesse James, the Dalton gang, Billy the Kid, and Flo Quick – were chased by lawmen like Wyatt Earp and Wild Bill Hickok, and everyone rode a horse.

Leather chaps, or trousers

Leather stirrups

The Appaloosa with its distinctive spotted coat (pp.40–41) was a favourite mount of native Americans

Cowgirl in typical Western clothes riding 14-year-old skewbald Cob

STAMPEDE!
Every July at the Calgary Stampede in Canada, the contests of skill and speed at this rodeo include the dramatic chuck (food) waggon races. Two pairs of horses, a cook/driver, and four outriders race around a circuit - the first across the finish line wins.

Lasso for roping cattle

Stetson

Saddle horn

Silver and tooled leather gunbelt

HOLLYWOOD HEROES
"There isn't a bronc that can't be rode; there isn't a cowboy that can't be throwed." The central feature of the rodeo show is the bucking horse, symbol of a man's need to subjugate the wild and the free, but a horse is not "broken" without a fight. Wild horse races are also a feature of the rodeo, in which terrified, unbroken horses are saddled and ridden to show off the cowboys' courage. Movie cowboys and their famous horses – such as the Lone Ranger and Silver, Roy Rogers and Trigger – helped to recreate the legend of the Old West.

Western curb bit

BUFFALO HUNT
In this painting by American artist George Catlin (1796–1872), the native Americans' horses are shown hunting the buffalo – which all but disappeared from the West through excessive slaughter by European immigrants.

PAUL REVERE'S RIDE
Famous for his ride from Boston on the night of 18 April 1775 to warn the colonists of Massachusetts that the British troops were coming, Paul Revere (1735–1818) and his borrowed horse have become an American legend.

ARMY ROUGHRIDERS
Ordinary cavalrymen (an army's mounted forces) had to spend long hours in the saddle, so it was important to have strong horses. In this painting by the American artist Frederic Remington (1861–1909), the US Cavalry is in hot pursuit.

Leather chaps

Leather stirrups

Cowboy on Palomino (part Thoroughbred, part Arab)

Sporting horses

Every year in Siena, Italy, horses and riders race around the main square in the dramatic and exciting *Palio*

"**T**HEY RAPIDLY FLEW OVER THE PLAIN, swiftly … whilst their manes were tossed about by the breath of the wind." This description of a chariot race comes from Homer's *Iliad* (written in the eighth century BCE), in which five Greek warriors raced across the plain of Troy in honour of the hero Patroclus, killed in the Trojan War. In the seventh century BCE four-horse chariot races were part of the early Olympic Games, while in later centuries the Romans raced horses in a "circus", or special arena. From the end of the Roman Empire, sports with horses went into a decline that lasted until the Middle Ages. Then, in the late 11th century, the first flat racing began in England, and later, in Renaissance Europe, riding schools teaching classical equitation developed. In 1750 the first Jockey Club was founded in England, and by 1775 trotting races began in Russia. Today, competitive sports with horses are as popular as ever, and huge amounts of money are invested in breeding racehorses.

Circus horse by French painter Georges Seurat (1859–1891)

Pommel

Cantle

Metal stirrup

A smooth leather English saddle has a very low cantle and pommel

There is a legend that Pelops, here driving a four-horse chariot, founded the Olympic Games in 1222 BCE to honour the supreme deity, Zeus

Hard hat

Format riding jacket

Throatlash

Running martingale

Browband

Checkpiece

Noseband

Numnah

Seven-year-old dapple grey jumper – a mix of Irish Draught and Irish Thoroughbred

Painted wooden barrier at least 1.4 m (4.5 ft) high

POINT TO POINT
Steeplechasing began in 1752 as a cross-country race in which a church steeple was the goal and all the hedges, or gates, in between had to be jumped to reach it.

OVER THEY GO
To jump over obstacles in their path is part of the natural behaviour of wild horses that are galloping away from a predator. But domesticated horses will only jump when directed to do so by their riders. To train a horse to be a show jumper is a long and complicated process.

IN COLD WATER
Three-day eventing tests the endurance, speed, and obedience of a horse, as well as its rider's ability. The event is broken down into dressage on the first day, followed by a cross-country / steeplechase course that includes a spectacular water hazard (as shown), with show jumping on the third and final day.

FUN FOR EVERYONE
Mounted games, or gymkhanas, offer young riders a chance to see what they and their ponies can do at this junior level of equestrian, or horseriding, competition.

Riding side-saddle originated with European royalty some 600 years ago, but in 19th-century England ladies rode in this way for the hunt

Saddle horn

High cantle

Lariat

Leather stirrup

Rein

Classic jodhpurs, or riding pants

English jumping saddle

Western saddles, made of heavy tooled leather, had distinctive pommels (saddle horns) used by cowboys when roping cattle with lariats (lassos)

Bridoon

Tendon boots to protect from overreach of hind feet

Girth

Metal stirrup

ANYONE FOR POLO?
Polo, as seen in this 17th-century silk print, was invented by the Chinese about 2,500 years ago. Today it is very popular in Argentina, the USA, Australia, and Britain. Two teams of four players each hit the ball with long-handled mallets and try to score as many goals as possible in seven and a half minutes (a "chukka"). There can be from four to six chukkas in a match. The team with the most goals wins the match.

THEY'RE OFF!
Modern flat racing – racing on a track with no obstacles – owes its existence to the Thoroughbred (pp.38–39), first developed in Britain during the 17th and 18th centuries. Today influential racing nations include Britain, France, Italy, Australia, and the USA.

59

Horses for courses

THE CLOSE BOND that has been forged over thousands of years between humans and horses cannot be broken by the rise of the motor car. Today the horse is becoming ever more popular in competitive sports, and those who cannot take part in showjumping or racing get much pleasure from watching them on television. Most highly bred horses, in particular those that compete at the highest levels, must be carefully trained to maintain their fitness and optimise their chance of winning. Racehorses will use their natural instincts to follow a leader (the other horses), helped by the sting of a whip. Show jumpers and dressage horses combine training with obedience. Besides racing or jumping, the most ancient sport involving horses is hunting, which many people consider to be cruel to the prey. Horses (singly or in teams) provide an amazing variety of sport and recreation for thousands of people around the world – from pony-trekking and endurance racing to international driving and classical equitation, or dressage.

AWAY TO THE RACES
Flat racing – the "Sport of Kings" – is very popular around the world with such classic races as England's Derby, America's Belmont Stakes, and Australia's Melbourne Cup. Here, the French impressionist painter, Edgar Degas (1834–1917), shows jockeys and horses in their owners' racing colours awaiting their call to the start line.

Height at withers 152 cm (15 hh/60 in)

CROSSING A CREEK
All around the world, pony-trekking is a popular recreation for both adults and children. In this picture, children are riding their ponies in single file across a shallow stream in the Victorian Alps in southeastern Australia.

PACERS AND TROTTERS
In many parts of the world, including North America, France, Russia, Australia, and New Zealand, the trotting, or harness, race is just as popular as flat racing. The modern trotting race has something in common with the ancient chariot race, except that it is run with a single horse that is only allowed to trot. In pacing (as shown here), the legs move in lateral (same side) rather than diagonal pairs (legs move in diagonal pairs for conventional trotting).

THREE HORSEMEN
For centuries, riders took part in long-distance races to see who could break the latest time and distance record. In this 18th-century Japanese print by Katsushika Hokusai (1760–1849), three horsemen are racing to the foothills of Mount Fuji.

Three-year-old bay American Standardbred driven by owner in his racing colours

ELEGANT DRESSAGE
Classical riding shows the horse at its peak of fitness and its obedience to its rider, and it reached its height of popularity in the 18th century. In modern advanced dressage competitions, marks out of ten are given for excellence. One of the most difficult movements (shown here) is piaffe, in which the horse maintains the beat of a slow, elevated trot without moving forwards.

For centuries, horsehair from the horse's tail has been used for stringing bows of musical instruments, such as the cello

HAVE YOU PASSED YOUR DRIVING TEST YET?
At horse shows around the world, driving events are very popular. In 1970, the first international horse driving trials, based on the format of the three-day event, took place. These trials had presentation and dressage on the first day, followed by a marathon of 27 km (17 miles), and then obstacle driving on the final day.

THE HUNTERS RETURN
Hunting from horseback has been carried out since the time of the Assyrians, c. 2500 BCE, when the prey was lions or wild oxen. Later, in Europe, as shown in this 16th-century Flemish calendar, the quarry was the stag, bear, or hare. In the 17th century, the English developed fox-hunting with the help of specially trained scent hounds.

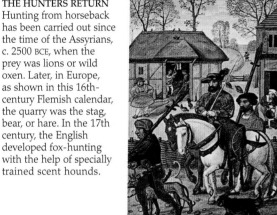

Driving whip

jockey cap

Shirt showing owner's racing colours

Sulky, or cart

Special harness around legs to help horse maintain its lateral pacing

Walking the horse

The horse has four natural gaits – the walk, trot, canter, and gallop. The walk has four beats – left hind, left fore, right hind, and right fore legs, each hitting the ground separately. The trot has two beats – left hind and right fore together, then right hind and left fore together. The canter has three beats – left hind, then left fore and right hind together, and finally the right fore leg. The gallop has four beats – the same as the walk – then all four feet come off the ground.

Useful ponies

CHILDREN WHO LEARN TO RIDE and look after a pony develop an understanding of the rich relationships that can exist between humans and animals, and a pony can often be a child's best friend. In the past, the native ponies of northern Europe were used as pack animals and for general farm work, and then when a particularly docile pony was too old to work, it was given to a small child for the first riding lessons. In those times almost everyone knew how to handle a horse. Today, fewer people learn to ride and even fewer have a pony of their own, but for those who do, it is a most rewarding experience. Most breeds, like the Dartmoor and Fell ponies, are extremely hardy and have evolved in a harsh environment where they survive on little food and remain outdoors all winter. However, thoroughbred ponies that are trained for the show ring need much more care.

THROUGH ALL KINDS OF WEATHER
From Missouri to California, Pony Express riders braved bad weather, difficult terrain, and attacks from native Americans to carry the post 3,300 km (2,000 miles) across the USA in the 1860s. They managed to cut delivery time from weeks to just days.

SMALL BUT MIGHTY
Shetland ponies were first bred as farm animals and, despite their very small size, they can draw a heavily loaded cart.

Pair of black Shetland ponies hitched to a cart loaded with hay and a bag of feed

RIDING FOR THE DISABLED
All disabled people who want to ride a horse should be given a chance to do so. Here a young rider is directing her pony with her feet, by reins attached to the stirrups.

How to look after your pony

To be responsible for a pony is very hard work, as the animal's welfare is entirely dependent on its owner. The pony must be given pasture, fresh water, and shelter, and it has to have regular exercise and constant companionship. It also has to be groomed and inspected for parasites, and its hooves have to be attended to.

Straw for bedding

Nourishing mix of barley, oats, maize, pony nuts, Spanish beans, and molasses

Sugar beet (must be soaked for 12 or 24 hours before feeding)

Rolled barley

A blue-glazed toy showing a boy and his pony, found in Egypt, c. 200 CE

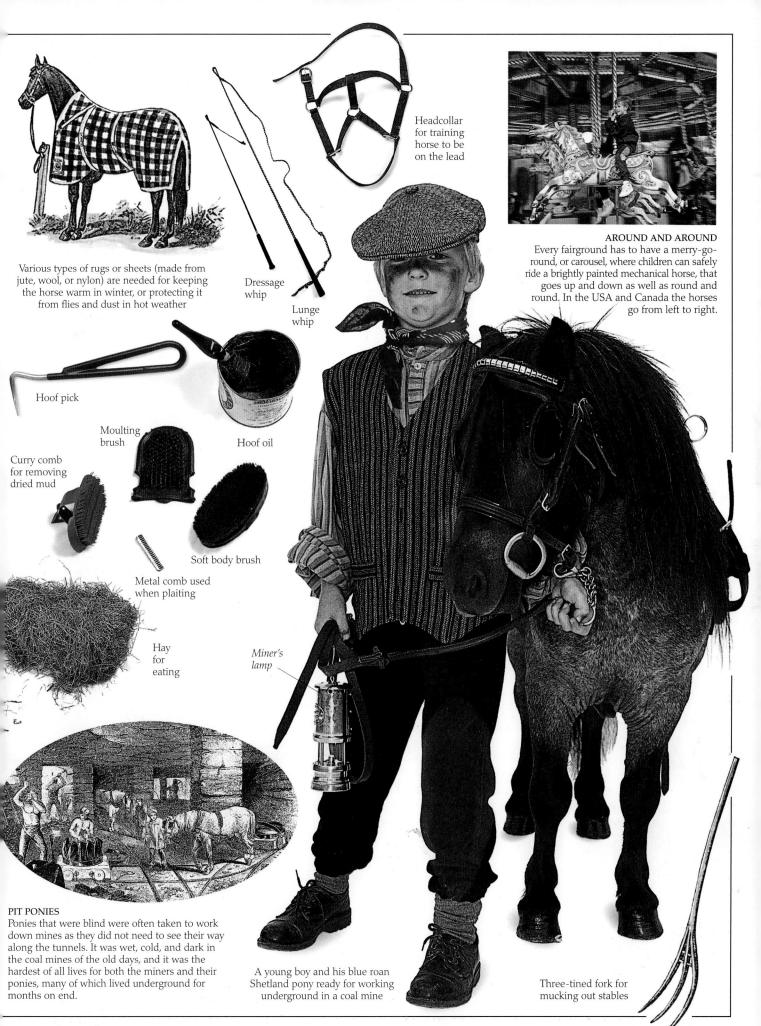

Various types of rugs or sheets (made from jute, wool, or nylon) are needed for keeping the horse warm in winter, or protecting it from flies and dust in hot weather

Dressage whip

Lunge whip

Headcollar for training horse to be on the lead

Hoof pick

Moulting brush

Hoof oil

Curry comb for removing dried mud

Soft body brush

Metal comb used when plaiting

Hay for eating

Miner's lamp

AROUND AND AROUND
Every fairground has to have a merry-go-round, or carousel, where children can safely ride a brightly painted mechanical horse, that goes up and down as well as round and round. In the USA and Canada the horses go from left to right.

PIT PONIES
Ponies that were blind were often taken to work down mines as they did not need to see their way along the tunnels. It was wet, cold, and dark in the coal mines of the old days, and it was the hardest of all lives for both the miners and their ponies, many of which lived underground for months on end.

A young boy and his blue roan Shetland pony ready for working underground in a coal mine

Three-tined fork for mucking out stables

Did you know?

AMAZING FACTS

The head of this herd of horses is probably a mare

A horse drinks at least 25 litres (44 pints) of water each day. That's about 13 times as much as an adult human.

Within an hour of being born, a foal is up on its feet and able to walk. It takes a child about a year to master the same skills. In the wild this ability is essential, because the foal has to move on with the rest of the herd.

A herd of horses is usually led by a mare (a female horse). She decides when the herd should move on to look for fresh grazing and also keeps discipline within the herd. She uses behaviour like the bite threat (see p.13) to keep the other members of the herd in order.

The "horsepower" is an internationally recognized unit of the pulling power of an engine. Scientists define it as the power that is required to lift a weight of 75 kg (163 lbs) over a distance of 1 m (39 in) in 1 second. But a real horse is 10 to 13 times as strong as this, so strangely one horse does not equal one horsepower.

People argued for many years about whether a horse takes all four feet off the ground when it gallops. Then in 1872, a photographer called Eadweard Muybridge set up a line of 24 cameras and photographed a horse galloping past. The pictures proved that during each stride a horse does indeed have all four feet off the ground at the same time.

A donkey carrying a load of straw

"Doing the donkey work" means doing hard, boring work. The expression comes from the fact that donkeys were bred for their stamina and endurance and were used mainly to carry heavy loads. More interesting jobs, such as carrying riders, were normally done by horses.

A 20-year-old horse shows its teeth

A mother horse and her foal

Horses have powerful lungs and strong hearts to help them run fast. A thoroughbred horse's heart can weigh up to 5 kg (11 lbs). That's about 16 times as heavy as an adult person's heart, which weighs in at a puny 300 g (9 oz).

The Shire Horse is the largest breed of horse. But the biggest-ever horse was a Percheron called Dr Le Gear. He measured an amazing 21 hands (213 cm/84 in) high.

The expression "straight from the horse's mouth" means to hear something directly from the best authority. It comes from the fact that the best way to discover the age of a horse is to examine its teeth. As a horse gets older, its incisor teeth become worn down and protrude out of its mouth more. Horse experts can use these signs to tell how old the horse is.

QUESTIONS AND ANSWERS

Q Why do newborn foals look so gangly?

A When a foal is born, its legs are already about 90 per cent of their adult length, whereas the rest of its body has to grow a lot. This makes it look very gangly. Foals often have to bend their front legs to reach down to eat grass.

Q Why are horses' eyes positioned on the sides of their heads?

A This eye position gives the horse good all-round vision, which is vital for spotting potential dangers. When a horse is grazing, it can see all round without having to raise or turn its head.

Q Why do horses often roll on the ground?

A Rolling helps a horse to scratch places it can't otherwise reach and to shed loose hairs from its coat. Horses from one herd usually roll in the same place. Each horse leaves its individual scent on the rolling patch. These scents gradually mix together to produce a unique "herd smell" that helps the horses in the herd to bond together.

A horse rolling

Q How fast can a horse run?

A The maximum recorded speed for a galloping horse is 69 km/h (43 mph). This is quick enough to put the horse among the 10 fastest mammals in the world, but it is way behind the fastest animal on earth, the cheetah, which can reach speeds of 105 km/h (65 mph).

A newborn foal

Q How did the Przewalski's horse get its unusual name?

A The Przewalski's horse is named after the man who discovered it – Nikolay Przhevalsky. He was a 19th-century Russian explorer who went on several journeys around east-central Asia, exploring previously little known regions, such as the Tien Shan Mountains and Lake Baikal. Przhevalsky was interested in wildlife and assembled extensive plant and animal collections. His natural history discoveries included the wild camel and the wild horse, which he found in western Mongolia in the 1870s.

Record Breakers

HIGHEST JUMP
The world record for the highest horse jump is 2.47 m (8 ft 1.25 in) by Captain Alberto Larraguibel Morales riding Huaso.

SPEED RECORD
The fastest winner of the Epsom Derby was a horse called Lamtarra, who completed the 2.4-km (1.5-mile) course in just 2 minutes 32.31 seconds in 1995.

BIGGEST BREED
The largest breed of horse is the Shire Horse, which stands 16.2–17.2 hands (165–175 cm/65–69 in) high.

SMALLEST BREED
The smallest breed of horse is the Falabella, which is just 7.5 hands (76 cm/30 in) high. Despite its small size, the Falabella is technically not a pony, but a miniature horse, because it has the characteristics and proportions of a horse.

Shire Horse

Q Why do horses run away?

A Horses facing danger have two options - fight or flight. They nearly always prefer to run away. One horse in the herd is always on guard. If it senses danger, it alerts the others and then the whole herd will run off. Horses run first and ask questions later!

Q When was horse racing first invented?

A The first records of a ridden race come from the ancient Greek Olympic Games in 624 BCE It took place over a distance of about 1,200 m (1,313 yds) and the jockeys rode bareback.

Q Why do horses come in so many different shapes and sizes?

A People have created the many different types of horse by selective breeding. This means limiting breeding to selected animals, perhaps by cross-breeding between different types of horse or in-breeding within a family. This is done to achieve a desired shape or skill. For example, some horses have been bred for strength, and others for speed. Gradually, over many years, a variety of distinctive horse and pony breeds have emerged from this process.

Falabella

Identifying breeds

THERE ARE ABOUT 160 DIFFERENT breeds and types of horse around the world. Many breeds were developed for specific purposes, such as riding, farm work, or pulling heavy loads.

PONIES

Each horse's height is given in hands (see p.7), next to the hand symbol.

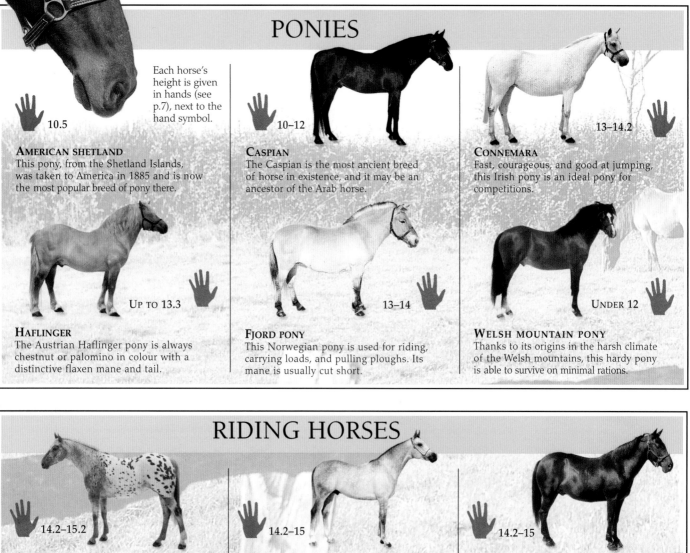

10.5

AMERICAN SHETLAND
This pony, from the Shetland Islands, was taken to America in 1885 and is now the most popular breed of pony there.

10–12

CASPIAN
The Caspian is the most ancient breed of horse in existence, and it may be an ancestor of the Arab horse.

13–14.2

CONNEMARA
Fast, courageous, and good at jumping, this Irish pony is an ideal pony for competitions.

UP TO 13.3

HAFLINGER
The Austrian Haflinger pony is always chestnut or palomino in colour with a distinctive flaxen mane and tail.

13–14

FJORD PONY
This Norwegian pony is used for riding, carrying loads, and pulling ploughs. Its mane is usually cut short.

UNDER 12

WELSH MOUNTAIN PONY
Thanks to its origins in the harsh climate of the Welsh mountains, this hardy pony is able to survive on minimal rations.

RIDING HORSES

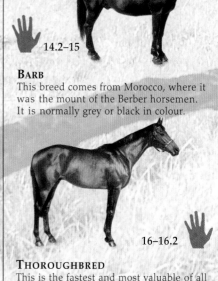

14.2–15.2

APPALOOSA
This horse has a distinctive spotted coat. It is descended from horses brought to the Americas by the Spanish conquistadors.

14.2–15

ARAB
The Arab is the purest breed of horse. It comes from the Arabian peninsula, where it was in existence as early as 2500 BCE.

14.2–15

BARB
This breed comes from Morocco, where it was the mount of the Berber horsemen. It is normally grey or black in colour.

14.3–16

QUARTER HORSE
This was the first American breed of horse. It was used for farm work and herding cattle and made a perfect cowboy's horse.

15.3–16

SELLE FRANÇAIS
This horse's name means "French saddle horse". It was bred for riding, and today is used for show jumping and racing.

16–16.2

THOROUGHBRED
This is the fastest and most valuable of all the breeds of horse. The Thoroughbred is used primarily for racing.

DRIVING HORSES

CLEVELAND BAY
16–16.2
Bred in the northeast of England, the Cleveland Bay was used to carry heavy men out hunting and to pull carriages.

FRIESIAN
15 AND OVER
This horse from the Netherlands was often used to pull funeral carriages because of its black colour.

GELDERLANDER
15.2–16.2
Bred specifically to pull carriages, this Netherlands horse is often used in carriage driving competitions.

HACKNEY
15–15.3
The British Hackney has a distinctive high-stepping gait. It was bred to pull carriages, especially the famous Hackney Cab.

LIPIZZANER
15.1–16.2
The white Lipizzaner horse is used at the Spanish Riding School in Vienna, where it excels at displays of dressage.

STANDARDBRED
15.2
This American horse is the world's best breed for harness racing. It can cover 1.6 km (1 mile) in under two minutes.

DRAUGHT HORSES

ARDENNAIS
15–16
Originating from the Ardennes region of France and Belgium, this is the oldest of the European heavy breeds.

BELGIAN DRAUGHT
16.2–17
This horse was originally bred for farm work. It has relatively short legs, but is noted for its great strength.

CLYDESDALE
16.2
The Clydesdale originates from Scotland. It was used for pulling heavy loads in cities, particularly brewer's drays.

PERCHERON
16.2–17.2
The French Percheron has been used for many tasks – pulling coaches, farm work, riding, and as a war horse.

SHIRE HORSE
16.2–17.2
The Shire Horse, from the middle shires of England, is the world's largest breed of horse. It was used for pulling ploughs and other farm work, and in cities for pulling brewer's drays.

Find out more

If you would like to get more involved in the world of horses, there are lots of ways to do it. You could start by visiting a horse show – there are many events held around the country in spring and summer, and indoors during the winter – or a county show where many breeds of horse are often on display. If you are feeling more adventurous, why not try going riding? Once you have mastered the basics, you will soon be able to go pony trekking in the countryside, or even enter a local competition yourself.

ROSETTES
Rosettes are given to the winners in riding competitions. In the UK, red signifies first place, blue second, yellow third, and green fourth. Tricolour rosettes, like this one, are presented for championships.

Tricolour rosette

You must wear a hard hat at all times when riding.

VISITING A HORSE SHOW
You can see horses taking part in sports such as show jumping, dressage, and driving events by visiting a horse show. Shows range from small local events, such as a riding club's gymkhana or a local point-to-point (steeplechase), to big county and international shows. The best known are listed in the "Places to Visit" box.

GOING RIDING
If you'd like to try riding, it is important to go to a proper riding school to learn. The British Horse Society produces a list of approved schools and can help you find one in your area. You won't need any special equipment, as the school will provide you with a hard hat, but it's a good idea to wear long trousers and a long-sleeved top to protect your skin if you fall off.

Knocking down this pole would incur four faults.

Jodhpurs are more comfortable for riding than ordinary trousers.

EQUIPMENT
After two or three lessons, if you decide you want to carry on riding, you could invest in some riding clothes. The first and most important things to buy are a hard hat and some riding gloves.

USEFUL WEBSITES

- Website for the British Horse Society (BHS), including lists of approved local riding schools, events, and information about breeds
  www.bhs.org.uk
- Website for the Pony Club, including calendar of events and competitions
  www.pcuk.org/
- Dates of horse shows around the country, good for finding small local events
  www.horsedates.co.uk
- Website of the National Horseracing Museum
  www.nhrm.co.uk/
- Information about the Horse of the Year Show
  www.hoys.co.uk/

Pony club silver trophy

Two Camargue horses

All Camargue horses are the same grey colour. Younger animals may be darker, but their coats lighten with age.

Fly fringes over the horse's ears help to cut out distracting sounds.

SEEING HORSES IN THE WILD
Several breeds of pony live wild in the UK – in the New Forest in Hampshire, and on Exmoor and Dartmoor in Devon and Somerset. Most of these ponies are owned by local breeders, but they are not used to contact with people, or dogs, so you should be careful not to get too close and frighten them. Further afield, herds of wild Camargue horses live in the Rhone delta region in the south of France.

Shire Horses pulling a plough

SEEING DIFFERENT BREEDS OF HORSES
Your local county show is a good place to see various types of horse, from ponies to hacks, hunters, and cobs. A large number of breeds are also on display at The Equine Event, held each year in Warwickshire. Abroad, you can see Andalusian horses at Jerez in Spain, and Lipizzaners at the Spanish Riding School in Vienna or at their stud in Piber, near Graz in Austria.

Places to Visit

INTERNATIONAL HORSE SHOWS HELD IN THE UK
- Badminton three-day event, Gloucestershire every May
- The Windsor Horse Show, Windsor, Berkshire every June
- Royal International Horse Show, Hickstead, Surrey every July
- Burley three-day event, Lincolnshire every September
- Horse of the Year Show, Wembley, London every October
- Olympia Horse Show, London every December.

NEWMARKET, CAMBRIDGESHIRE
The town of Newmarket is the centre of British horse racing. Top sights to see include:
- The National Horse Racing Museum, which tells the history of horse racing and has a large collection of sporting art
- The National Stud, where many British race horses are bred. You can see stallions, mares in foal, and possibly a new-born foal - most likely in April or May
- racehorses are exercised on the heath surrounding the town in the early morning.

THE ROYAL MEWS, LONDON
The Royal Mews is a working stable that houses the Queen's horses and the coaches that are used on state occasions.
Star exhibits include:
- the glass coach used for royal weddings
- the ornate gold state coach, built in 1762.

THE EQUINE EVENT, STONELEIGH PARK, WARWICKSHIRE
You can see more than 30 different breeds of horse on display at this event, which takes place each November. Other attractions include: displays and riding demonstrations, famous riders, and trade stands displaying all the latest products.

THE KENTUCKY HORSE PARK, LEXINGTON, KENTUCKY, USA
A working horse farm at which you can see around 50 different breeds of horse. Includes two museums, parade of breeds, and demonstrations of the farrier's skills.

L'ECOLE NATIONALE D'EQUITATION, SAUMUR, FRANCE
The French national riding school, famous for its *Cadre Noir* team. In the summer, you can visit the team's quarters, watch a training session, and see a dressage display.

A racehorse being excercised on Newmarket Heath

Glossary

ARAB One of the oldest of all the breeds of horse. Arab horses originate from the Arabian peninsula, where they were bred by the Bedouin people around 3,000 years ago.

ASS A member of the horse family. There are three types of ass – the African wild ass (*Equus africanus*), and Asian wild asses (*Equus hemonius* and *Equus Kiang*).

BARB One of the earliest breeds of horse. The barb comes from North Africa, and is the traditional mount of the Berber people.

BIT The part of a bridle that fits in the horse's mouth. Different styles of bit include the snaffle, the curb, and the pelham (see pp.31).

BLAZE A white marking on a horse's head. A blaze is a wide stripe which starts above the eyes and extends to the muzzle.

BRAND A mark burned on to a horse's skin to show its breed or who owns it.

BRIDLE The headgear used to control a horse. A bridle consists of leather straps round the horse's head, a bit in its mouth, and the reins that the rider holds.

BRUMBY A type of feral horse found in Australia. Brumbies are descended from domesticated horses that were abandoned during the gold rushes, 150 years ago.

BURRO A type of feral donkey first introduced into the desert southwest of North America by the Spaniards in the 1500s.

CANTER A gait in which the horse's feet hit the ground in three beats – the left hindleg, then the left foreleg and the right hindleg together, and finally the right foreleg.

CHIVALRY A combination of qualities expected of an ideal knight in the Middle Ages, such as courage, honour, and courtesy. The term comes from the French word *cheval*, meaning "horse", because knights were mounted soldiers.

COLDBLOODS The name given to an ancient group of horses from northern Europe. Modern-day heavy or draught horses, such as the Shire Horse, Percheron, and Jutland, are believed to have descended from these horses.

Bridle

COLT A male horse that is less than four years old and has been castrated.

CROSS-BRED An animal produced by breeding between two different members of the horse family, or between two different breeds of horse. For example, a mule is bred from a horse and a donkey.

CRUSADES A series of military expeditions made by European knights in the Middle Ages to capture the Holy Land (modern-day Israel) from the Muslims.

DOMESTICATION Donkeys were first domesticated in western Asia and Egypt about 6,000 years ago, followed by the beginnings of horse domestication in Asia and eastern Europe.

DONKEY A domesticated ass, descended from the African wild ass (*Equus africanus*).

DRAUGHT HORSE A horse used for pulling heavy loads and working the land, rather than for riding.

DRESSAGE A form of competition in which a rider shows off a horse's skills in obedience and deportment.

EQUIDS Members of the horse family of mammals, which includes domestic horses, wild asses, and zebras. The name "equid" comes from *Equidae*, the Latin name for this group of mammals.

EQUITATION The art of horse-riding.

FARRIER A person who shoes horses.

FERAL An animal that is descended from domesticated ancestors, but has returned to live in the wild. North American mustangs and Australian brumbies are examples of feral horses.

FETLOCK Part of a horse's leg that sticks out just above and behind the hoof. A tuft of hair often grows at the fetlock.

FILLY A female horse that is under four years in age.

FLAT RACING Racing horses on a track with no jumps or other obstacles.

African wild ass

FORELOCK The tuft of hair that grows on a horse's forehead.

GALLOP A fast gait in which the horse's feet hit the ground in four beats, and then all four feet briefly come off the ground at the same time.

GAUCHO A cowboy from the South American pampas. Gauchos use horses to round up their cattle.

GELDING A castrated male horse.

HAME Two pieces of curved wood or metal, fastened to the collar of a draught horse.

HAND A unit of measurement used to work out the height of a horse. One hand is 10.16 cm (4 in). A horse's height is measured from the ground to the top of its shoulders.

HARNESS The equipment of straps and fittings by which a horse is fastened to a cart or other vehicle and controlled.

HINNY An animal produced by interbreeding between a horse and a donkey. A hinny has a horse father and a donkey mother.

HOOF The horny part of a horse's foot. Hooves are made of keratin, the same substance as human hair and finger nails.

Dressage

Mane

HORSEPOWER A unit of power used to measure the pulling power of an engine. One horsepower is the power required to lift a weight of 75 kg (163 lbs) a distance of 1 m (39 in) in one second and is equal to 746 watts.

HOTBLOODS The Thoroughbred and eastern breeds of horse, such as the Arab and Barb. The name comes from the hot countries of North Africa and Arabia where these breeds originated.

JENNY A female donkey.

JOUST A combat between two knights mounted on horses and armed with lances. Jousting was a form of sport invented in the Middle Ages to allow knights to practise their fighting skills without actually killing one another.

Thoroughbred

LIGAMENT A short band of fibrous tissue that links two bones together and allows a joint to move freely.

MANE The long hair that grows from the back of a horse's neck.

MARE A female horse who is four or more years old.

MULE An animal produced by breeding between a horse and a donkey. A mule has a donkey father and a horse mother.

MUSTANG A type of feral horse found in North America. Mustangs are descended from domesticated horses brought to America at the end of the 15th century by the first European settlers.

MUZZLE A horse's nose and mouth area.

ONAGER Another name for the Asian wild ass (*Equus hemonius*).

PACE A lateral, two-beat gait in which the two legs on the same side of the horse move forward together.

PACK ANIMAL An animal used to carry loads, rather than for riding. Mules have often been used as pack animals.

PIEBALD A colour of horse's coat in which there are large, irregular patches of black and white.

POINTS The external parts of a horse, such as its poll, pastern, withers, and fetlock.

PONY A horse that is less than 14.2 hands (147 cm / 58 in) high.

PRZEWALSKI'S HORSE The only surviving kind of wild horse. Przewalski's horses became extinct in their homeland on the Mongolian steppe during the 1960s, but they are now being reintroduced there from herds bred in captivity.

RODEO A competition in which North American cowboys show off their skills at riding horses and handling cattle.

SHOW JUMPING A sport in which horses are ridden around a course which contains a number of fences to jump. The contestants are given penalty points, called faults, for any errors.

SIDESADDLE A position for riding a horse in which both the rider's legs are on the left side of the saddle. In former times, women often rode sidesaddle because their long skirts prevented them from sitting astride the horse.

SKEWBALD A colour of horse's coat, in which there are large white patches on another coat colour.

SPUR A U-shaped device with a small spike or wheel attached. Spurs are fitted to the heels of a rider's boots and are used to urge a horse forward.

STALLION A male horse who is four or more years old, and has not been castrated.

STEEPLECHASE A race over fences and open ditches. Traditionally, a steeplechase was a crosscountry race from one village to another.

STEPPE A huge grassy plain stretching across Russia and Mongolia. The steppe was once home to herds of wild horses.

STIRRUPS Two leather loops suspended from a horse's saddle with metal footrests to support the rider's feet.

STRIPE A white marking on a horse's head. A stripe is a long narrow strip which extends from above the eyes to the nostrils.

A South American spur

TERRET A ring on a saddle harness through which the driving reins pass.

THOROUGHBRED A horse whose ancestry can be traced back to one of three famous stallions – the Byerley Turk, the Darley Arabian, or the Godolphin Arabian.

TRACE Each of the two side straps or chains by which a horse pulls a vehicle.

TROT A gait in which the horse's feet hit the ground in two beats – the left hind and right foreleg together, then the right hind and left foreleg together.

WALK A slow, four-time gait in which each of the horse's legs hits the ground separately.

WARMBLOODS A name used to describe breeds of horse which are crosses between hotbloods and coldbloods. The Trakehner and the Hanoverian are examples of warmbloods.

WHIPPLETREE A crossbar used to attach a horse's harness to a waggon.

WITHERS The top of a horse's shoulders.

ZEBRA A member of the horse family, found in Africa, which has a coat patterned with black and white stripes.

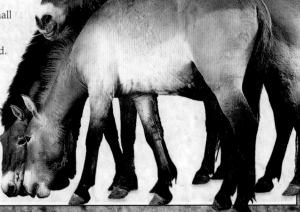

Przewalski's horses

Index

Acknowledgements

Dorling Kindersley wish to thank:
Alan Hills, Dave Gowers, Christi Graham, Sandra Marshall, Nick Nicholls, and Barbara Winters of the British Museum, and Colin Keates of the Natural History Museum for additional special photography; Clubb Chipperfield Limited, Foxhill Stables & Carriage Repository, Suzanne Gill, Wanda Lee Jones of the Welshpool Andalusian Stud, Marwell Zoological Park, the National Shire Horse Centre, Harry Perkins, and the Whitbread Hop Farm for lending animals and vehicles for photography; The Household Cavalry for providing the rider and the drum horse, and The Knights of Arkley for the jousting sequence; The Berrriewood Stud Farm, Carol Johnson, and Plough Studios for their help in providing arenas and studios for photography; Dr Alan Gentry of the Natural History Museum, Christopher Gravett of the Royal Armouries (HM Tower of London), and Rowena Loverance of the British Museum for their research help; Kim Bryan for editorial consultancy; Céline Carez, Hannah Conduct, Liz Sephton, Christian Sévigny, Helena Spiteri and Cheryl Telfer for editorial and design assistance; Jane Parker for the index; Stewart J. Wild for proof-reading; David Ekholm–JAlbum, Sunita Gahir, Susan Reuben, Susan St. Louis, Lisa Stock, and

Bulent Yusuf for the clipart; Neville Graham, Sue Nicholson, and Susan St. Louis for the wallchart.

Illustrations: John Woodcock

Picture credits:
t=top, b=bottom, c=centre, l=left, r=right

Aerofilms: 21tl.
Allsport: 58tr Vandystadt; 59br Ben Radford.
American Museum of Natural History: 8cl, 9br.
Ardea: 14clt, 14cl, 16c, 17cr Jean-Paul Ferreo, 17bl Joanna van Grusen.
Barnaby's Picture Library: 43cr, 45bl.
Bridgeman Art Library: 41tl Archiv fur Kunst & Geschichte, Berlin; 34bl Biblioteca Nacional, Madrid; 24tr, 51cbr, 60c British Library; 49tl Guildhall Library; 39cb Harrogate Museums and Art Galleries; 35t, 41tl, 56tl, 59tc Private Collection; 57ct Smithsonian Institution, Washington, DC; 32bl Musée Condée, Chantilly; 58tl (detail) Musée d'Orsay, Paris; 60tr (detail) Louvre, Paris.
Trustees of the British Museum: front cover tl, 4ctr, 7br, 16tl, 17br, 22tl, 22cl, 22br, 23tr, 26c, 28c, 33tr, 33bl, 46bl.
Bruce Coleman Ltd: 12bl C Hughes; 18b J.

& D. Bartlett; 39tl C. Henneghien.
Mike Dent: front cover cr, 23tl, 27tl, 46ctl, 50tr, 54cl, 63tr.
Dorling Kindersley: 37tr Dave King (by courtesy of the National Motor Museum, Beaulieu); front cover, 27tr, 36tl, 38 (all except 38br), 40bl, 41 (all except 41 tl, 41 br), 50c, 50–51 b, 51tr, 51cl, 51cr, 56bl, 63bc Bob Langrish.
Mary Evans Picture Library: 23bl, 32tr.
Robert Harding Picture Library: 21cr, 24cb, 48tr, 51be, 56cr.
Alan Hills: 20bl.
Hirmer: 33tl.
Michael Holford: 31tc, 44tl, 47tc, 59bl, 60bl.
Hulton Picture Collection: 53b, 63bl.
Kentucky Horse Park, U.S.A 67cb.
Frank Lane Picture Agency: 12br.
Bob Langrish: 13c, 20bl, 37tl, 40br, 41br, 54cr, 56cl, 57t, 58bc, 59tl, 59tr, 61tl, 61tc, 65br, 66–67.
Jim Lockwood, Courage Shire Horse Centre, Berks. 67bl.
The Mansell Collection: 42bl.
Peter Munt, Ascot Driving Stables, Berks 67tr.
Prince D'elle, Haras National De Saint Lo, France, 66bc.
Natural History Photographic Agency: 14br Patrick Fagot; 21br E. Hanumantha Rao; 36bl, 60cl A.N.T.
Peter Newark's Western Americana: 34tr, 34cl, 43tl, 48cb, 55tl, 57cb, 57bl, 62t.
Only Horses: 37c, 62bl.
Oxford Scientific Films: 17tc/Anup Shah/Okapia.

Planet Earth: 19br Nick Greaves.
Pegas of Kilverstone, Lady Fisher, Kilverstone Wildlife Park, Norfolk. 65br;
Spin way Bright Morning, Miss S. Hodgkins, Spinway Stud, Oxon 66tr.
Ann Ronan Picture Library: 6tr.
The Board of Trustees of Royal Armouries: 2c, 43cl, 45tc, 45cr.
Whitbread Brewery: 13cr.
Zefa: 12tr, 13tr, 24tl, 24bl, 25cr, 35br, 36cl, 46cb, 52cl, 52br.

Wallchart:
The Trustees of the British Museum: tl

All other images © Dorling Kindersley
For further information see:
www.dkimages.com